The **ALPHA** Equestrian
CHALLENGE

U

Becoming **A** *Leader* **P***repared to* **H***andle* **A***nything*

Nelly Cooper

Outskirts Press, Inc.
Denver, Colorado

The opinions expressed in this manuscript are solely the opinions of the author and do not represent the opinions or thoughts of the publisher. The author has represented and warranted full ownership and/or legal right to publish all the materials in this book.

The Alpha Equestrian Challenge
Becoming a Leader Prepared to Handle Anything
All Rights Reserved.
Copyright © 2014 Nelly Cooper
v2.0

This book may not be reproduced, transmitted, or stored in whole or in part by any means, including graphic, electronic, or mechanical without the express written consent of the publisher except in the case of brief quotations embodied in critical articles and reviews.

Outskirts Press, Inc.
http://www.outskirtspress.com

ISBN: 978-1-4787-2486-5

Library of Congress Control Number: 2013920513

Outskirts Press and the "OP" logo are trademarks belonging to Outskirts Press, Inc.

PRINTED IN THE UNITED STATES OF AMERICA

CONTENTS

A Message to Riding Instructors

Developing good horse leadership skills is absolutely vital to the safety of your students. Despite years of riding lessons, I had no idea I was missing out on this crucial part of rider education until I was kicked in the head by a horse. This near-death experience motivated me to seek out information on my own to teach myself how to get horses to behave calmly.

In the years since, I have been helping others develop their own leadership skills. Unfortunately, most of my students come to me only after they've been frightened and/or injured by their horses.

Too many of us find out the hard way that we can't just learn to ride; we must learn to be good leaders to our horses as well. The majority of rider injuries, rider fear and dangerous horse behavior can be prevented if students learn *from the start*:

- that they need to be good leaders to their horses;
- how to be good leaders to their horses; and
- how to prevent their horses from reacting dangerously out of fear.

Helping your students develop these three skills is exactly what this challenge is all about, and your leadership as their instructor is vital to their success.

Leadership skills are first built on the ground and then carried to the saddle. To become good leaders, your students must learn to work with their horses effectively on the ground. If teaching groundwork is not something you enjoy or have time for, I encourage you to explore other options. You could team up with someone who loves teaching students on the ground. Why not have a ground skills instructor at your barn? There are many people who would love to fill that position. Some of them, like myself, have spent years helping students who have been unnecessarily scared or even injured by the horses they so wanted to enjoy.

If you choose to teach the groundwork yourself, there are many ways to go about it. You can teach one or two exercises each week; or devote the first half of each lesson to groundwork until the student becomes proficient; or perhaps devote one lesson a month exclusively to groundwork. Explore your options to find a way that really suits you and your lesson program.

It doesn't matter whether you choose to teach the groundwork or have someone else do it. What matters is that your students become confident leaders on the ground so they can carry that confidence into the saddle. By learning to deal with their horses' challenges on the ground, students can establish leadership and get their horses' calm submission prior to mounting. Encouraging your students to conduct groundwork before riding gets their rides off to a much safer start. As the instructor, it's important you monitor each student's progress to ensure each student's success. To do that you must get your students in the habit of doing groundwork before each ride, and get yourself in the habit of taking a few minutes before each lesson to evaluate them.

Students that have gained some skill at groundwork exercises are ready for bomb-proofing. A lot of folks think bomb-proofing is just for desensitizing the horse so it won't get distracted from doing its job. That way of thinking puts it on the horse to take care of the rider. If horses were cool with this, I'd have no reason to write this book. Horses are prey animals with an instinctual fight or flight response to danger. Bomb-proofing is really about honing a rider's ability to focus so *she* won't get distracted from doing *her* job, which is leading her horse safely through this big, scary world! Nothing builds better leadership skills quicker than bomb-proofing.

Bomb-proofing provides the perfect way to teach students how to prevent their horses from bolting. These skills need to be started on the ground and constantly evaluated to determine when the student is ready to start bomb-proofing in the saddle. I encourage you to incorporate frequent bomb-proofing exercises into your riding lessons so students learn to stay aware of their horses' body language and to respond quickly and confidently in any situation to keep themselves and their horses safe. Prepared students can show their horses that this big world isn't so scary after all.

Lastly, bring your students' parents into the mix. Many parents love hanging out at the barn helping their children get ready for lessons and shows, visiting with other parents, or just admiring the horses. They want to be helpful, but many of them are intimidated by horses. These parents have no idea that their own behaviors might very well have a negative effect on the behavior of the horses their children are about to ride. For instance, many coddle nervous horses not knowing that it only makes those horses more nervous. Or they give treats when horses behave impatiently not knowing that they are creating pushy behavior. Help these parents be helpful. Why not book a parent night every now and then? Teach them something about horse behavior and safe horse handling. They will love you for it.

Leadership education is vital to every rider's safety. However you choose to go about teaching it, what matters most is that **none** of your students miss out on it.

Equipment Needed for
The **ALPHA** Equestrian Challenge

- A lead rope with a chain (in addition to your horse's regular halter.) Detachable chains are available if your lead doesn't have one. I recommend cotton leads because, to me, they have the best feel and grip. If you use a lead other than cotton, wear riding gloves to prevent painful rope burns.

- Dressage whip up to 42" long.

- Halter training whip (54-60" long) with a plastic flag taped to the end. Cheap disposable table cloths work great for this purpose.

- Tarp, roughly 6x8 feet.

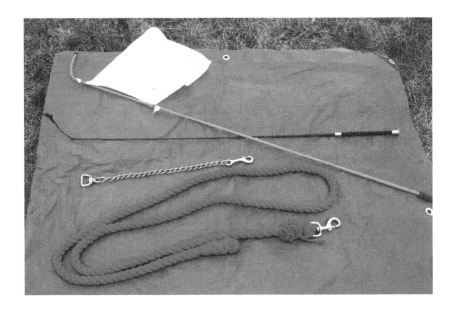

A Message to Riding Students

Being a good rider is not the same as being a good leader. Good riding skills allow you to have fun in the saddle. Good leadership skills allow you to keep your horse calm and cooperative so your fun time doesn't turn into a terrifying experience. Riding and leadership are two completely different sets of skills that, when combined, make horseback riding a blast. But there's no way you can learn the leadership part by sitting in the saddle.

Riders who don't learn this early on often wind up getting hurt and scared by their horses. That's because we're not riding bikes here. We're riding large, powerful animals that have brains and instincts and fear. Lots and lots of fear. Bikes don't have fear because bikes aren't prey animals. No predator goes hunting for bikes because bikes aren't delicious. It sounds creepy to think of a horse as tasty, but that's exactly what predators do and horses know it. That's where all their fear comes from in the first place.

Bikes never get scared and freak out. Lots of horses, on the other hand, freak out on a regular basis. On a bike, all you have to do to stay safe is to stay balanced. You have to stay balanced on your horse, too, and just about anybody can balance on a calm horse. A freaked out horse is a whole different story. Even the best riders are hard pressed to stay on a horse that's in panic mode. When you ride your horse, your safety depends more on your ability to keep your horse calm than on your actual riding skills.

For a horse to behave calmly it must feel safe. If your horse does not feel safe with you when you're standing next to him on the ground, he's not going to suddenly change his mind about it when you climb in the saddle. Becoming a good leader is all about making your horse feel safe with you *all the time* so he can calmly do what you want him to do, even when you're riding.

Although it is important that you meet your horse's physical needs, providing food, shelter and health care is not what makes your horse feel safe. Likewise, loving him with all your might does not make him feel safe either. You make your horse feel safe by giving him the same type of fair, firm leadership an alpha mare would give.

To develop leadership skills, you must start on the ground and then carry those skills into the saddle. Under the guidance of your riding instructor, this book will get you started:

- By gaining a clear understanding of how horses think and behave, you can start making your horse feel safer with you in all of your moments together.

- Developing groundwork skills will allow you to get your horse's calm submission to your leadership before you climb in the saddle.

- Through bomb-proofing exercises, you can build your horse's confidence in your leadership so you can prevent him from behaving dangerously out of fear.

Good leadership not only keeps you and your horse safe, but it is the best gift you can give your horse because it's what allows him to enjoy his time with you. Develop your leadership skills so you can put your riding skills to use and start having the time of your life with your horse.

A Message to Parents

I encourage you to read this book along with your child. Your behavior around the barn affects the behavior of the horse your child rides. Gaining a basic understanding of horse behavior will empower you to have a positive rather than negative effect.

I would also encourage you to get with the instructor and book a lesson or two of your own to learn how to handle a horse safely and confidently. The benefits to both you and your child are more than worth the price of these lessons. Even something as simple as holding the horse while your child runs to the restroom can quickly turn into an intimidating experience if you're not prepared.

Developing a few leadership skills of your own will help you enjoy the time you spend around horses and will help your child have a safer riding experience.

If it isn't challenging,
it isn't leadership.

Chapter One

A LEADER PROVIDES HERD ASSURANCE

Until you become the leader of your horse, he will be, believe it or not, the leader of you. You must depend on him to keep you safe. You can't rely on that forever because there is only so much your horse is comfortable doing as the leader. While you are learning to ride, your horse is depending on you to take over the responsibility of leadership so that you can keep him safe.

You might think your horse will never behave dangerously because he is too well-trained. Yet, riders get scared and injured by well-trained horses on a regular basis. As a riding student, you need to understand that the trainer's job is to *get* your horse behaving calmly so he becomes safe for you to ride, but it is your job to *keep* your horse behaving calmly so he remains safe for you to ride. If you don't reinforce the training you will actually undo the training.

You might think, too, your horse will never behave dangerously because he is just naturally laid back. No matter how laid back a horse is, he is still a prey animal. When in fear, he will buck or bolt just like any other horse. If you have a naturally laid back horse, your job is to help him stay that way.

Then there are horses that are so high-strung you might think they are incapable of calm behavior. Trainers with good leadership skills can prove otherwise because they understand that anxious horses don't have any self-confidence. As these horses develop confidence, they too become calm, well-trained horses. Your instructor will do her best to match you with the right horse for your level of confidence. However, it is your job to help your horse maintain his self-confidence by working to build your own.

When you ride your horse you have to boss him around to get him to do stuff. Bossing around your horse while you're riding him does not automatically make you his leader. Your horse knows that you are not the leader, but he has been trained to carry a rider and he will allow you to boss him around as long as you keep him within his comfort zone.

Your horse's comfort zone is made up of all the stuff *he* feels safe doing as the leader. How much stuff that might be completely depends on the amount of self-confidence your horse has. Older horses that have seen and done lots of things generally have wider comfort zones than younger horses that haven't experienced as much, or horse's that have had lots of bad experiences.

Now here's the deal about your horse's comfort zone:
- The longer you ride your horse without taking on any leadership responsibility, the smaller your horse's comfort zone becomes with you. This means that you might get your horse to do something one day, but you might not be able to get him to do that same thing a month later. The sooner you become the leader, the more stuff you'll be able to get your horse to do.

- As you become a better rider you will naturally ask more of your horse. You will start pushing him to the limits of his comfort zone, which will start freaking him out. If you push him over the edge, he'll blow up on you and start bucking, bolting or rearing. The sooner you become the leader, the more stuff you can get your horse to do without him scaring or injuring you.

Your horse can keep you safe only as long as he feels safe with you. You become the leader by making your horse feel safe with you all the time. Once you have taken over the responsibility of leadership, you won't have to worry about your horse's comfort zone because he will trust you to lead him safely through new experiences.

Chapter Two

A LEADER UNDERSTANDS HER POSITION
AS HERD ALPHA

Just as your horse was not trained overnight, you're not going to become a good leader overnight. You're going to face a lot of challenges along the way. Simply put, a challenge from a horse is any behavior that confuses you, annoys you, frightens you, hurts you, or has the potential to hurt you.

Pushing you around with his head, jerking his head back when you try to put on the halter, fidgeting around during grooming, pawing the ground, kicking his stall, dragging you around on the lead rope, running away from you in the pasture, moving away from you when you try to mount, refusing to move forward, stopping to scratch his leg when you've asked him to trot, crowding your space, spooking at ridiculous objects, turning his butt to you in the stall, biting at other horses, nipping or biting at you, barreling into you to avoid another horse, kicking, bucking, rearing, bolting, etc. – all of these confusing, annoying, frightening, painful and potentially injury-causing behaviors are challenges.

Challenging behavior is normal horse behavior. If you watch horses in the pasture, you will see them challenge each other every now and then. They annoy each other, frighten each other, and sometimes hurt each other. But, the one thing they never do is confuse each other because horses understand that the nipping, biting, kicking, bucking, and rearing are all very normal horse behaviors.

Horses are driven by instinct to challenge each other because this is what causes them to mature both physically and mentally. Young horses spend lots of play time presenting challenges to other horses to develop muscle, speed, courage and confidence. This challenging process ensures the herd members grow to be fast and strong and brave enough to venture into new areas in search of food. Without the challenging process, horses could never have survived as a species of prey animals.

As the young horses grow and become bigger and stronger, all their playing around starts to hurt. If playing were allowed to go on and on, it would jeopardize the health of the herd. Tired, wounded prey animals are easy pickings for predators; so horses have to learn to behave calmly to stay safe.

Just as challenging behavior is very normal horse behavior, calm behavior is also normal horse behavior. In fact, among themselves, mature horses spend most of their time behaving calmly. They still challenge each other occasionally to make sure the herd stays strong, fast, and courageous. Each horse will challenge another from time to time just to make sure they're all still on top of their game.

To get calm behavior, horses have to make each other settle down and mind their manners. The horses who get really good at this float to the top of the pecking order; they become the leaders—the alphas. To become your horse's leader, you have to get really good at making him mind his manners.

It's important you understand that your horse can't treat you differently because you are a human. Horses can only think and behave like horses. What that means for you is that your horse will treat you as if you were just another herd member. He will present you with calm behavior, and he will present you with challenging behavior.

Since challenging behaviors are annoying, frightening and often painful, we humans tend to think of them as "naughty" behaviors. But in truth, challenging behavior is very normal horse behavior just as calm behavior is very normal horse behavior. They are two sides of the same coin. We humans have a knack for getting upset by the one side, yet taking the other side completely for granted. Hopefully, this book will give you the wisdom to try your best to do neither.

The job of a horse trainer is to deal with all the dangerous challenges a horse may present when it begins working under saddle. The trainer then takes the horse through lots of different experiences to expand its comfort zone. As the horse gains confidence in himself and his surroundings, he gets comfortable doing things as the leader.

Once he gains enough self-confidence, a horse is ready to take on a student rider. At this point, your horse is already used to having humans in the herd. You just have to get used to acting like a herd member so you can take over leadership of your herd, which consists of you and your horse. Whenever you are together, you and your horse are your own little two member herd.

Because you are now a herd member, your horse will challenge you at some point. It's important you understand that when your horse challenges you it isn't because there is something wrong with him, or because he's mean, or because he does not like you; he's only challenging you to find out if you're on top of your game. There is never any reason to take it personally; he's just checking to see if you're a confident herd member so he can decide who's in the lead.

You always have the choice of whether or not to take the lead, but if you decide not to, you force your horse to be the leader. There is no neutral position. Either you take the lead or your horse will have to. When making your choice, keep in mind that the leader has two very important jobs:

1. **The leader is responsible for making the other herd member mind his/her manners.** A horse makes another horse mind its manners by biting, kicking, rearing and all kinds of other painful stuff. This is how horses treat each other. Your horse can only behave as a horse, so he can

only treat you like another horse. If your horse has to make you mind your manners, he could easily injure you. Your horse can't give you a timeout because you're a human. However, you can make him mind his manners without ever injuring him.

2. **The leader is responsible for the safety of the herd, so the leader makes all the decisions about danger.** Horses are notoriously awful at determining exactly what's dangerous and what's not. A mailbox, a plastic bag, a bicycle, an umbrella, a funny sound, a flower pot, a hose, a bird, a saddle pad hanging on a fence - to horses, all of these things (and soooooo many more) are potential predators waiting to attack! If your horse is forced to make the decisions about danger, he's going to spend a lot of time looking around for danger, spooking at things he thinks are dangerous, and probably bolting away from lots of them. You, however, already know that just about everything you're going to encounter presents no danger at all, so wouldn't it be best if you made these decisions?

I'm going on the assumption that you have wisely chosen to be the leader. As the leader, you must deal with your horse's challenges in a way that proves to him you are the leader. Each time you deal with a challenge effectively, you get calm behavior from your horse.

YOUR ALPHA RESPONSIBILITIES:

1. Make your horse mind his manners.

2. Make all the decisions about danger to keep you and your horse safe.

Chapter Three

A LEADER'S POWER is in HER ATTITUDE

For you to answer any challenge correctly, you have to respond in a way that convinces your horse that you are the leader. That means you have to start thinking and acting as a lead horse would think and act.

Watch a pasture full of horses and you'll start to see that the lead horse is not necessarily the biggest and strongest. The lead horse is simply the one who's best at making the other horse's mind their manners. Quite often a little pony is the leader over herd members twice its size. The larger animals gratefully accept her as leader because her small size means nothing to them. Her attitude means everything.

So what is it about the pony's attitude that makes her such an appealing leader to a bunch of bigger, stronger horses? Three things:

1. **She is always aware.**
2. **She has the greatest sense of self-preservation.**
3. **She is by far the most stubborn.**

Now remember, a larger horse can only determine if the pony is the leader by challenging her: by annoying her, scaring her, or hurting her. So, let's take a closer look at a challenge to see how the pony's attitude makes her the leader.

Pretend a bigger horse has decided to challenge the pony by biting her on the rear end. He starts his challenge by moving toward her. The pony is **always aware**, so she senses the horse moving toward her. She understands this is a challenge and she's ready for it.

She might be afraid because the horse is so big, but she's faced a few challenges before and has gotten hurt in the process. She knows very well that if she doesn't stick up for herself, she will get hurt again. Her **sense of self-preservation** overrides any fear she may be feeling as she deals with the challenge. Knowing the horse can't hurt her unless he actually makes contact with her body, she protects her space, with all her might if need be.

So here's how the pony responds to the challenge: First she'll pin her ears to warn the horse to back out of her space. If he doesn't, she'll lunge at him as if she's going to attack him. If the horse doesn't back away then, she will go after him full force and lay into him with her teeth and hooves. She will keep at it for as long as it takes to make him back down and mind his manners because she is **by far the most stubborn**. This is how the pony proves she is the leader.

For you to become a good leader, you have to develop these same qualities within yourself.

DEVELOP YOUR ALPHA QUALITIES:

1. Awareness

2. Great sense of self-preservation

3. Stubbornness

Chapter Four

A LEADER POSSESSES HEIGHTENED AWARENESS

Be aware that you need to be the leader of your horse because he has a limited comfort zone, which means there is only so much he is comfortable doing as the leader. Taking over leadership is what allows you to safely expand your horse's comfort zone.

Be aware that you are supposed to develop your leadership skills as quickly as possible so that you can take over the leadership from your horse as quickly as possible. Don't make him beg you to do your job.

Be aware that leadership is a full time job that starts the moment you go get your horse from his stall or pasture and doesn't end until you put him back in his stall or pasture. You have to be the leader the entire time you're with your horse, not just when you're riding him.

Be aware that leadership comes with two main responsibilities:

1. You are responsible for making your horse mind his manners.
2. You are responsible for the safety of the herd, so you must make all the decisions about danger.

Be aware that you must show your horse that you are capable of protecting yourself, and therefore him. You will learn more about this in the next chapter.

Be aware that, before climbing into the saddle, you should always do groundwork with your horse to prove to him that you are the leader, and to allow him the opportunity to calmly submit to your leadership.

Be aware that every time your horse presents you with any behavior that you find confusing, annoying, frightening or painful,
he is presenting you with a challenge. The more you ask him to
do, the more he will challenge you to become a better leader;
therefore, you must improve your leadership skills as you improve your riding skills.

If you provide your horse with good leadership all the time,
your horse will behave calmly despite any pain and fear, despite
its gender or breed, despite its past history or anything else. It's
true! So many riders never come to understand how true this is
because they allow all of these things to become reasons, therefore excuses, for challenging behavior.

For example, suppose your horse starts acting balky under saddle, maybe giving little bucks or flailing its head around. You
check him out and determine that he might be in pain, so you
call the veterinarian, chiropractor, massage therapist, saddle-
fitter, or whoever else you need to call to relieve your horse's
pain. Many riders would just leave it at that feeling like they
have done everything they should do. They are wrong and will
always have horses that balk or buck when in pain because they
have not addressed the challenge.

Horses tell us they are in physical pain by presenting sick, sore,
wounded behavior: limping, laying down, trying to rub their
bellies, avoiding food and/or water, bleeding, coughing, moving
stiffly, acting lethargic; or by twitching, shrinking, or jerking
away to avoid pressure on a wound or sore spot, etc. Horses tell
us they are in need of better leadership by presenting annoying,
frightening, painful or potentially painful behavior—challenges.

Be proactive about your horse's physical health and comfort. If
you think he is wounded, sick, or sore, call whoever you need to
call to relieve the pain. But understand that veterinarians, chiro-
practors, or other equine professionals cannot provide your

horse with the leadership he needs from you for his mental well-being. Be proactive about your horse's mental health by recognizing challenges when they are presented and dealing with them effectively. Help him stay emotionally fit by helping him feel more secure with your leadership.

Another very common example is spookiness. Many riders experiment with feed changes, calming supplements and devices such as ear plugs, nose guards and fly bonnets, hoping one of these things will cure the spooking. There is no cure for spooking because it is not an illness or a disease, a mental defect, or a breeding trait. It is only a challenge, and the only way to make it stop is by dealing with the challenge effectively. Use all the calming supplements, ear plugs, and nose guards you want while dealing with the challenge, but don't let your use of these things prevent you from dealing with the challenge effectively. Once you've dealt with it effectively, you will no longer need the calming supplements.

Horses that are provided good leadership consistently do not behave dangerously when they are afraid. They have no reason to because they trust their leaders to protect them and keep them safe from harm. If your horse is spooky, he is challenging you to become a leader he can trust to keep him safe. Take your horse through bomb-proofing exercises to allow him the opportunity to build confidence in your leadership. Prove to him that he does not have to worry about his safety when he is with you, and he will calmly allow you to lead him through any situation.

Get a clue! Horses can't talk so they can't tell us when we need to improve our leadership skills. They can only give us clues through their behavior. Start listening to yourself and to the other riders around you, and you will start to see just how many clues horses give us.

My horse won't let me put on his halter. My horse is just fine unless he hears something behind him. My horse doesn't like it when I brush back by his hind legs. My horse won't stand still long enough to let me braid. My horse doesn't like me touching his ears. My horse is scared of plastic bags. Don't put my horse on the crossties because he'll freak out. My horse won't go in the wash bay because he's scared of the drain. Ugh, my mare is in season; this isn't going to be any fun. I can't ride down there because my horse is afraid of the door. He always bucks when he needs his hocks injected. It wasn't my horse's fault that the cat jumped out right then. My horse is just so curious about everything. Will you help me catch my horse? My horse is so afraid of whips somebody must have beaten him. Watch my horse; he has a tendency to bite. I was having the best ride until that other horse started freaking out (or until that car alarm went off, or until my horse caught sight of that flag, umbrella, or baby stroller.) What does my horse keep looking at? I think I'll lunge my horse to get his bucks out. A car came by and my horse just freaked out and took off. Why does my horse always have to poop in the aisle?

Every single one of these statements and questions, and the million others like them, is a clue that some horse in the barn is looking for better leadership. (That last one may have stumped you, but trust me, it's a clue.) When you find yourself thinking or saying things like this, it's because your horse is presenting you with a challenge. Be aware and accept the challenge to become a better leader before you or someone else has to say, "Call 9-1-1."

Be aware that as you take on the responsibility of leadership, you allow your horse to be the follower. What's a follower's job? A follower's job is to pay attention to the leader! So, much of your work as a leader will be telling your horse, "Hey, mind your manners and pay attention to me."

Chapter Five

A LEADER PROTECTS HERSELF ASSERTIVELY

Protect Your Space: Your horse must have a healthy fear of you to willingly accept you as his leader. In fact, it's impossible for you to be a good leader to your horse *without* establishing within him a healthy fear of you. In case you haven't noticed, horses are huge. It takes hardly any effort at all for a horse to run over you. Horses have giant bulk and giant force. All they have to do is aim it in your direction to cause you severe injury.

When it comes to the relationship between you and your horse, there is nothing more important than proving to your horse that you will do whatever it takes to protect yourself from him. Why? Because if you can't protect yourself from your horse, how on earth will he ever believe you can protect *him* from anything?

There are times when it's absolutely necessary to be mean and scary to make your horse respect your space. Many people think we are supposed to be nice to horses and gentle with them all the time in order to be respectful of the horse. I used to believe this myself, and then I got kicked in the head. That incident could very well have killed me. Others haven't been so fortunate.

I can't tell you how many times I've heard riders who have been bitten by horses say, "I couldn't hit him; I don't want people thinking I'm mean." We all need to start slapping each other just for saying that! When did defending our own bodies become horse abuse?

If you don't make your horse mind his manners and respect

your space, he will think he is the leader which means he will have to make you mind your manners. Remember, horses make other horses mind their manners by biting, kicking or rearing. This is not a joking matter. I've seen lips bitten off, cheeks bitten off, backs broken, feet crushed, fingers pulled off, numerous concussions and too many broken toes to count, all because riders were not making horses respect their space... all because they didn't want to be seen as mean. I would rather have someone think I'm mean than have my lip bitten off any day of the week.

To be a true leader to your horse, you have to do what's right for the horse and not worry about what other people think. If a horse hurts you, or even attempts to, you should reprimand him no matter who happens to be watching. If you don't, you are doing the horse a disservice. (If someone has a problem with that, you tell them to call me so I can slap them for being stupid!)

Horses want leaders, and when the chips are down, horses want leaders who are mean enough and scary enough to protect them from predators. Now, the chances of the two of you ever running into a predator are probably pretty slim, but your horse doesn't know that. Horses are prey animals and always will be. If they sense even the slightest hint of danger about anything, they will react as if it's a predator. They have to because this is how prey animals survive.

If a horse is in a herd when it senses danger, it is driven by instinct to shoulder up next to the closest horse to keep from being separated from the herd, because once a horse is separated from the herd... well, you know. You have to remember that your horse sees you as just another herd member, which means he'll try to shoulder up next to you. You will get crushed if you don't act quickly to prevent yourself from getting crushed. The only way to do that is to make him more afraid of *you* than whatever frightened him in the first place. You can't do that without getting mean and scary.

You can be a kind leader, and you can be a loving leader; but understand that if you don't make your horse respect your space, you are not being a leader at all.

If you still struggle with the idea of getting mean and scary on purpose, it will help you to understand that your version of mean and scary is nothing compared to a horse's version of it. Go back and re-read about the lead pony in Chapter Three. That pony, like all lead horses, had no qualms about charging at that larger horse, and biting and kicking him with all her might. Talk about mean and scary! She scared the bejeezies out of that horse, and he developed a very healthy fear of her.

You might be wondering, if the horse feared the pony, wouldn't he want to spend less time with her? Nope. Just the opposite. He would want to spend more time right by her side because he knows if a predator came along it would have to go through the pony to get to him. By guarding her space so closely, the pony established herself as a protector in the horse's eye. The horse then became willing to mind his manners so the pony would welcome him into her space.

Your horse will have to challenge you to find out how protective you are of your space. He will be counting on you to prove you can protect yourself and can, therefore, protect him as well. When, not if, there comes the time that you have to get mean and scary to force your horse to respect your space, understand that you are letting him down if you don't stick up for yourself in a major way. Protect your space to give your horse the gift of making it the safest place he knows... as long as he minds his manners.

Learn to Listen to That Little Voice Inside Your Head
We've all heard the old saying 'if you fall off a horse you have to get right back on.' Not necessarily. If you fall off because you lose your balance, sure you should get back up, and keep on getting back up until you learn to balance yourself well enough to stay in the saddle.

But, if you fall off because you lose control of your horse, you're probably going to feel a little bit scared about getting right back up. As well you should because you haven't done anything to lessen the chances of it happening again. To have fun and exciting lives we all have to overcome our fears, but there's no reason we have to be foolish about it. The easiest way to suck the fun out of riding is to allow yourself to get injured by climbing right back up on a horse you couldn't control just moments ago.

Fear is an extremely valuable gift because it is a warning. It would be great if it came with flashing red lights and clear voice calling out, "Stop! Don't do it!" But fear doesn't come with that stuff. It just presents itself as a bad feeling. Learn to trust it and let it motivate you to take some time to get more control of your horse on the ground. Take as much time as you need to convince yourself you can control the horse once you get back in the saddle. Whether that's minutes, hours, days or weeks, who cares? The time for you to climb back up is when you feel more confident than scared.

Only you know exactly how you feel, so don't let anyone pressure you into riding until *you* feel confident in your ability to control your horse. After all, it is your body. When you are on your horse, you are the only one who can protect it.

Chapter Six

A LEADER PERSISTS in HER ATTEMPTS

Sometimes it's really easy to get a horse to stop presenting a particular challenge, and sometimes it takes a huge amount of effort, courage, patience and time. Whatever the challenge, your horse's behavior will always serve as proof of whether or not you have been successful in dealing with it. There is only one way to fail, and that is by giving up before your horse gives up. The one sure-fire way to succeed is to be more stubborn than your horse.

Your horse is depending on you to be more stubborn because the leader is always the most stubborn. He will challenge you lots of times just to make sure you're more stubborn. Hold your ground until you get what you want. Period. Don't give up. This does not mean you have to spend hours dealing with one particular challenge. It just means you need to come back to it until you have dealt with it effectively.

Once a horse presents you with a certain challenge, he will continue to present the exact same challenge until you figure out a way to make him stop. Remember, horses challenge each other to develop both mentally and physically because they need their leaders to be quick and sharp. You will never be able to outrun your horse, but you can outthink him at lightning speed. By presenting you with the exact same challenge time and time again, your horse is giving you the opportunity to hone your mental acuity.

For example: you attempt to lead your horse out of his pasture and he challenges you by planting his feet and refusing to budge. You give him a tap with the lead rope and still he doesn't move. So, you tap a couple more times and eventually he moves and off you go. The next day, you attempt to lead your horse out of his pasture and he again plants his feet and refuses to budge - the exact same challenge as the day before. He'll do this every single day until you figure out a way to make him stop presenting this particular challenge to you. In other words, he'll get into the habit of presenting you with this challenge.

So be quick and sharp: recognize that when your horse develops a habit that gets on your nerves, it's only because you have been slow and dull in dealing with that challenge. Be quick and sharp: recognize that if you respond to a challenge and your horse keeps on presenting that challenge, you have to respond to it in a different way to be effective.

You don't have to get everything perfect all at once. Nobody can do that. Each day, you just have to try to deal with challenges better than you did the day before. Horses are big and intimidating, so it takes time to develop the confidence needed to be a really good leader. Everyone makes lots of mistakes along the way, so go easy on yourself and try not to get frustrated. It's perfectly OK to make mistakes. Your horse doesn't care how many mistakes you make, he only cares that you keep trying. He is counting on you to keep trying because he knows leaders never give up.

It's perfectly fine, and recommended for safety's sake, to have your instructor by your side while you're developing your confidence and skill at dealing with different challenges. But it is vital that *you* do the work so that *you* become the leader. If you feel too scared to deal with a particular challenge, ask your instructor to help you but come back to it and try to do it yourself after you've gained more confidence. Dealing with your horse's challenges is what makes you the leader. Hang in there for the long haul so you get to the point where you're perfectly comfortable dealing with any challenge your horse presents to you.

Chapter Seven

A LEADER PRUDENTLY HANDLES ANY ANTICS

Horses present all kinds of challenges to riders before they ever climb in the saddle. The following is a list of common challenges and suggestions on how to deal with each one effectively to make your horse mind his manners.

Remember, your horse's behavior is always the proof of whether or not you have dealt with a challenge effectively. For example: if you try to give your horse treats, and he challenges you by getting pushy and demanding about it, you will know you have dealt with the challenge effectively when he calmly accepts treats in a respectful manner.

LEADING

As a general rule of thumb, you should lead your horse with a chain over the nose band of his halter (as illustrated on the following page) until you're confident he will follow you calmly no matter where you go. Correct your horse with the chain by giving it a quick sharp jerk and release. Never just apply steady pressure to the chain because it won't have any meaning to your horse.

- **Challenge: Your horse moves too quickly and drags you along.** Correction: Make sure you lead with the chain fastened over your horse's nose. Once you begin walking, the first time he puts the slightest bit of pressure on the lead, give a quick hard jerk and release on the chain. The quick jerk and *release* is important. (Never just apply steady pressure because your horse will just push into the steady pressure and continue to drag you along.) The second time he

To apply the lead chain correctly, first insert the chain through the halter ring on the near side as Tina demonstrates in the top photo. Bring the chain under and over the nose band of the halter before attaching it to the ring on the far side. The final result should be as pictured below.

puts pressure on the lead, bring him to a halt by giving a much harder correction with the chain, and then make him back up a few steps. Keep repeating, making your corrections progressively more forceful until he understands he is to walk beside you with zero pressure on the lead.

- **Challenge: Your horse moves too slowly and lags behind you.** Correction: Keep yourself at his shoulder. Using your left hand, swing the lead rope behind you to smack his rear end prompting him to move more quickly. The first couple of times you do this, he will probably shoot right out ahead of you. That's OK. After a couple of strides, he'll go right back to trying to lag behind. Give him another tap on his rear end. Keep at it until he understands he's supposed to keep up with you, not the other way around.

- **Challenge: Your horse refuses to move forward.** Correction: Since it's easier for a horse to move forward than backward, you can use a little reverse psychology to deal with this challenge. Make your horse back up until he stops on his own, and then ask him to move forward. If he again refuses, make him back up several feet past the point where he would prefer to stop, and then ask him to move forward. If he again refuses, make him back up until he tries to avoid backing altogether by taking a step forward or sideways. (To save yourself time and energy, turn his rear in the direction you want to go before you start the backing process.)

- **Challenge: Your horse pulls the lead out of your hand and runs away.** Correction: Do not run after him because that will cause him to run faster and farther. He won't run far unless you give him reason to. Keep an eye on him by following him at a calm walk. When he stops, walk calmly up to him, pick up the lead and continue on about your business. This experience usually freaks a horse out, so there is no need to reprimand unless he gives you an indication that he is still not willing to follow calmly. In that case, give corrections with the lead chain until he follows calmly.

As Emily helps Olivia get better control of her pony, she is careful to allow Olivia to make the corrections so Justin comes to see Olivia as his leader. Bottom photo: Justin turns an ear toward Olivia as she brings him to a halt—a sure sign he is starting to pay attention to her.

Once Olivia gains some respect from Justin, Emily gives her full control of him as they continue their lesson. Top: Olivia learns to back Justin. Bottom: She cues Justin to move with her by tapping him with the lead rope.

23

Before: As leader, Justin had no problem dragging Olivia around.

*After: Olivia's now in the lead and has Justin's attention and calm coopera-
tion... and no pressure on the lead rope.*

- **Challenge: Turning his head away.** Correction: Before attempting to put the halter on, place the lead rope around your horse's neck and use it to prevent him from turning away from you.

- **Challenge: Lifting his head high and backing away.** Correction: Always halter from the horse's left side, facing the same direction he's facing. Use your right arm to hold your horse's head down as you put the halter on with your left hand. If needed, put pressure directly on his nose to prevent him from lifting his head too high. When he backs up, go with him guiding his hind end toward a wall to stop the backing process. If you're in the pasture, allow the fence or the lead rope around his neck to stop the backing, or keep following him backward until he stops on his own.

IN YOUR HORSE'S STALL

- **Challenge: Crowding your space.** Correction: As you enter the stall, move your horse out of your space using pressure on his face or chest. If you can't budge him, grab a whip or lead rope for reinforcement, and tap him on his chest progressively harder and harder until he moves backward. If you need to spend time in his stall (mucking, feeding, etc.), make him stay out of your space while you're in there, using a whip, lead rope, or even your rake for back-up if necessary. Many riders believe stalls are the horses' space and upon entering they must work around the horses rather than vice versa. Consequently, horses are very unmannerly when these riders are in their stalls. Providing good leadership is not a part-time job. Make your horse respect your space one hundred percent of the time, even when you're in his stall.

- **Challenge: Rushing to get out of the stall.** Correction: Be aware of your horse's body language when you approach his stall. If he looks nervous, he will try to rush out the moment you open the door. Open the door just a little way and

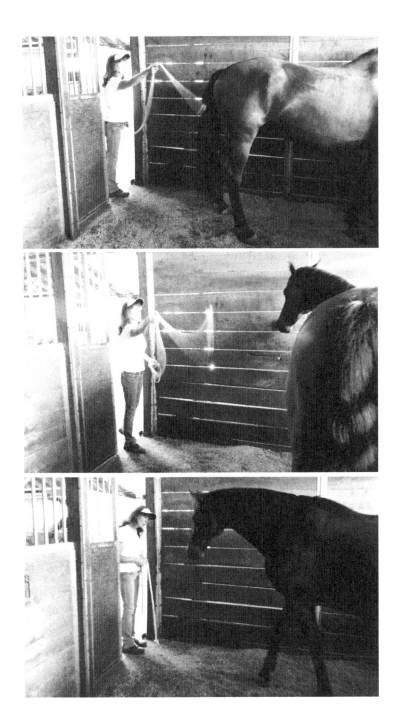

Standing safely at the door, Rena uses a lead rope to keep Izzy moving until he presents his front end rather than his hind end.

make him move out of your space as you enter to put on the halter and lead. Then, rather than just opening the door and leading him out, make him back up a couple of steps, then simply stand there. If he tries to move, give the chain a jerk or two, and again just stand there. Repeat until he stands completely still for several seconds, and then have him follow you out of the stall.

- **Challenge: Rushing to get into the stall.** Correction: Be aware of your horse's body language and do not allow him to speed up his pace as you approach the stall. If needed, bring him to a halt and make him stand a few seconds and be patient. When he crowds your space at the stall door, make him back up to allow you room to enter first. Be demanding about it. If he happens to rush into the stall ahead of you, pull him right back out and start over. Get in the habit of never allowing your horse to enter any doorway or gate ahead of you unless you invite him to do so.

- **Challenge: Turning his rear toward you.** Correction: Stay safely near the door and swing a lead rope into the stall toward your horse's rear end to cause him to move. If he does not turn to face you, keep swinging the lead making him move around *until* he turns to face you. The second he does, stop swinging the lead rope to let him know that's exactly what you want him to do.

FEEDING TIME

- **Challenge: Kicking the stall.** Correction: Horses will kick the stall to demand that you feed them instantly. If you feed them instantly when they kick, they will get more demanding and kick even harder. The trick to solving this challenge is in letting your horse know he's going to get fed when he's patient, not when he's kicking the stall. Keep a whip near his stall. When he kicks, pick up the whip and tap the stall door to let your horse know that kicking it isn't acceptable. Withhold the feed for two or three minutes and just wait. When he kicks the stall again, tap the stall door

Kyleigh carries a whip to keep Ice Baby respectful of her space while she feeds. Horses can be very pushy at feeding time, or they can be patient—but you must ask for their patience and demand it when necessary.

much harder. Again, withhold the feed and wait. If he kicks again, repeat the process. Get at least two minutes of calmness before feeding. If you're vigilant about reprimanding rather than rewarding the kicking, he will quit kicking the stall in just a few days.

- **Challenge: Crowding your space when you're trying to feed him.** Correction: Carry a whip or lead rope into the stall or pasture and use it to force your horse to go to the back of the stall while you dump his grain. If he moves, lunge toward him a little bit and say "whoa" very firmly, like you mean it. It only takes a second or two to feed, so he can be patient. But he won't be patient if you don't ask for his patience, or insist on it, or demand it if necessary.

- **Challenge: Rushing into his stall to get to his feed before you can take off his halter.** Correction: Drag his nose out of the feed and bring him back over to face the stall door. Make him stand there while you un-halter him. If he acts impatient, make him stand there longer. Un-halter only when he is standing perfectly calm. Again, he can be patient, but he will only be patient if you ask him to.

TURN-OUT TIME

- **Challenge: Once inside the pasture, your horse tries to take off before you can get the halter off.** Correction: Carry a treat in your pocket for a week or two. Have your horse back up a couple of times before entering the pasture. Be very stern about it to make sure he's minding his manners.

For a couple of days when you enter the pasture, turn your horse around to face the gate, and then give him the treat as you take his halter off. For three or four days, show him the treat but don't give it to him until you take his halter off. For several more days, keep the treat in your pocket until you take his halter off, and then give it to him. You can then start tapering off the treats by giving him one every other day, every third day, once a week, then not at all. By the time you're done, your horse will have forgotten about challenging you in this manner.

GETTING YOUR HORSE FROM THE PASTURE

- **Challenge: Running away from you.** Correction: First, as you approach your horse, don't try to get his attention by making clucking or smooching sounds because those are sounds we use to make horses move away from us. Secondly, put it in your horse's head that if he runs away from you he is going to have to run a lot harder than he originally wanted to. Follow him around and when he comes to a stop, swing your lead rope around and make some clucking or smooching sounds to make him run again. Keep doing this until he turns to face you when he comes to a stop. By turning to face you, he is letting you know he's tired of running. At this point, soften your posture and walk up to him very matter-of-factly, not hesitantly like a predator creeping up on him. Give him a nice rub on his neck to show him that you approve of his decision to stand still. If he happens to take off again, repeat the whole process.

- **Challenge: Other horses crowd your space when you're trying to get your horse out of the pasture.** Correction: Enter the pasture as the leader of all the horses, not just your own. Force other horses to respect your space just as you force your own horse to do. Use your lead rope to shoo the other horses away. If you feel like the lead rope isn't enough, it's perfectly OK to carry a whip to the pasture and use it to protect your space. Once your horse is attached to you by the lead rope, it is your responsibility as his leader to protect him. This is your golden opportunity on a daily basis to prove to him that you will protect him, so absolutely do not allow other horses to threaten him as you lead him out of the pasture. Using the tail end of your lead rope (or the whip), keep the other horses out of your space and make them back well away from the gate so you can get your horse out safely and calmly.

Kristen uses the lead rope to shoo the rest of the herd away from the gate so she can get her horse out safely. Enter the paddock as leader of all the horses, not just your own, and be prepared to protect your space.

31

- **Challenge: Your horse threatens another horse.** Correction: Once your horse starts feeling safe under your leadership, he might get a little full of himself and try to threaten other horses as you're leading him. Reprimand his behavior by giving a very sharp jerk and release on the lead chain. It is your responsibility, not his, to guard your space and he is never allowed to do that job for you.

- **Challenge: Your horse tries to rush out of the gate ahead of you.** Correction: Force him to back up and wait patiently while you exit the gate, then ask him to follow calmly. Be aware that your horse is more likely to present this challenge if you allow other horses to crowd the gate, so insist that they stay back and give you plenty of space. Again, use the tail end of the lead rope or a whip if necessary to guard your space.

GROOMING

- **Challenge: Your horse moves around or paws at the ground.** Correction: Lead him to where you want him to stand for grooming, make him halt and say "whoa." Keeping hold of the lead, begin grooming. When he moves, give a correction with the chain, put him back in place, say "whoa" and begin grooming again. When he moves a second time, give a much stronger correction with the chain, and so on. After a few corrections, he will get the hint that you want him to stand perfectly still.

- **Challenge: Your horse flails his head around when you touch his ears.** Correction: You should be able to touch and groom every part of your horse's body, but horses are very sensitive about their ears and many have their ears abused by twitching. Patient training or retraining is very important. Stand to the side of your horse to keep your feet out of harm's way. Holding onto the lead, get him used to your touch by firmly stroking his forehead and his poll, working your way all around the base of his ear. At the first sign of irritation, keep your hand firmly in place, hold him

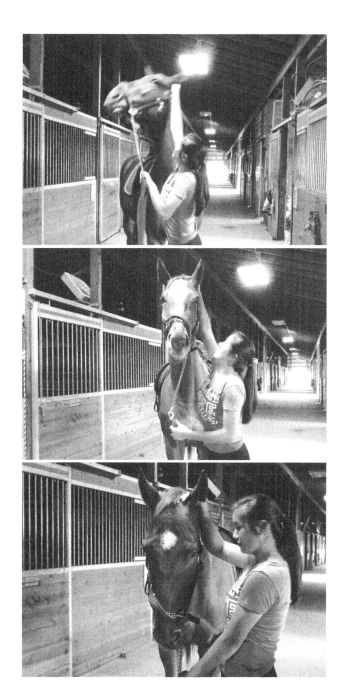

Top: Piper flails her head when Anna first tries to touch her ear. Center: Piper presents much less drama once she realizes Anna isn't phased by it. Bottom: By remaining patient and calm, Anna helps Piper learn to enjoy having her ears rubbed.

tight with the lead and ignore the fussiness. When he calms down, reward him by removing your hand and giving him a treat. Repeat the process and once your horse is used to your touch around the base of his ear, start moving your hand along the back of his ear. When he tries to lift and shake his head, keep his ear gripped firmly in your hand until he stops moving around. Again, reward the calmness by removing your hand and giving a treat. Practice with your horse in this manner and he will come to see having his ears touched as a positive rather than negative experience.

- **Challenge: Your horse gets agitated when you try to groom near his privates.** Correction: Again, the trick to dealing with this challenge is to remove your hand when your horse is calm, not when he's being fussy. Start getting him used to your touch by using your hand only. Keeping your touch firm, rub your horse under his girth area as if you were brushing him. Work your way backward, and at the first sign of agitation, keep your hand firmly in place and ignore his fussiness. As soon as your horse settles down, remove your hand. Once your horse is used to your hand, you can start using a soft brush to groom that area. If he acts fussy about the brush, repeat this same process until he calmly accepts it.

- **Challenge: Your horse won't pick up his feet for hoof picking.** Correction: First adjust your horse so he is not bearing weight on the leg you want him to lift. Ask him to lift his hoof, and if he tries to shift his weight back onto that leg, shift the weight back off the leg and say "whoa" in a firm voice. Give him a couple of chances, but then add a reprimand in the form of a quick pop on his hip or shoulder depending on which leg you're working with.

- **Challenge: Your horse tries to kick or jerk his hoof out of your hand during hoof cleaning.** Correction: Always make sure you stand against the side of your horse to allow him to lift his hoof straight up, not out. Lift the hoof higher than you normally would, hold on tighter than you normally would, and when you feel him try to kick or jerk say, "Knock it off," in a firm voice.

- **Challenge: Your horse always poops or pees in the aisle.** Correction: Horses' bladders and bowels are affected by nervousness and excitement. Taking over the responsibility of leadership has a calming effect on your horse—and his bladder and bowels. If your horse habitually poops or pees while you're getting him ready for riding, it's a good indication that you have not yet taken over leadership. Learn the groundwork exercises in the following chapter to move this process along. Then, do the leading and backing exercise with your horse as you lead him to the barn to allow him to see you as his leader prior to grooming and tacking up.

TACKING UP

- **Challenge: Your horse gets agitated when you tighten the girth.** Correction: Make sure your saddle fits and be fair about tightening the girth slowly. Try using treats to get your horse more accepting of the girth. First, get a feel for how tight the girth can get before your horse protests. Then, tighten the girth one hole below that point and give a treat. Tighten it one hole further. If he doesn't protest, give a treat. If he does protest, loosen it and try again. Only give a treat when he doesn't protest. Keep practicing with him like this for a few days. Then attempt to go up two holes at a time, and so on.

- **Challenge: Your horse backs away to avoid bridling.** Correction: Always put the reins over his head before removing the halter so you have something to hold him in case he really tries to get away. Bridle from your horse's left side facing the same direction he's facing. Hold the cheek pieces in your right hand and the bit in your left. When he starts backing, allow your right hand to put pressure on the center of his face to keep his head down as you back up with him. Guide his hind end so that he backs into

35

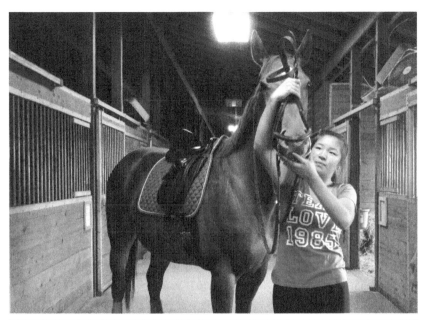

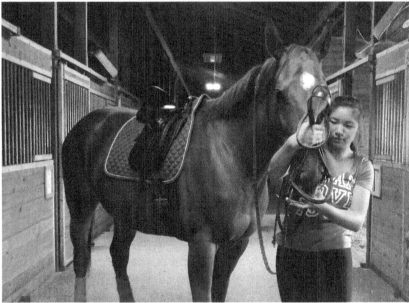

Horses will often back up and raise their heads to avoid bridling. Top: Anna finds that guiding Piper's hind end toward the wall is enough to stop her from backing any further. Bottom: Anna encourages Piper to lower her head by applying pressure to the center of her face.

a wall, and then put the bridle on. You could also sugar cubes to make bridling a positive experience for horses new to it. Place the sugar cube under the bit to encourage your horse to reach for it rather than back away from it.

- **Challenge: Your horse won't accept the bit.** Correction: It's important that you hold the bridle correctly and that you have yourself in the correct position for bridling. Holding the bit by his mouth, use a finger to massage the corner of his mouth until he unlocks his jaw and then slip the bit in.

GIVING TREATS

- **Challenge: Getting pushy about treats.** Correction: Your horse should accept treats respectfully. Many riders quit feeding treats when their horses start pushing them around to get the treats. Treats are a nice reward for a job well done. If your horse gets pushy about it, don't give up and quit giving treats. Just demand that your horse be more patient. Until you get really good at keeping your horse out of your space, only give treats when your horse is haltered with the chain over his nose. Pick up the treat, and when he moves into your space to get it, give the chain a very sharp jerk and release – hard enough to make him back up a step or two, and then make him stand there for a several seconds. If he moves toward you again, give another correction. When he is mannerly and still for several seconds, *you* move into *his* space and give him the treat.

ANYTIME

- **Challenge: Your horse nips at you.** Correction: When your horse nips at you, he is basically trying to make you mind your manners and leave him alone. Nipping is very dangerous because it leads to biting which can cause horrible injury. It's very important that you make your horse understand that he is never allowed to nip or bite you. To nip, your horse will normally swing his head right around to where your hand is. If you are quick enough, bop him hard

Through her body language (hand up, prepared to step or lunge toward the horses if necessary), Rena prevents the horses from crowding her space as she prepares to feed them apples. It's fun to give treats but it's important for horses to accept them respectfully.

38

in the mouth with the back of your hand. (Many people think if you hit a horse anywhere on his face it will cause him to become head-shy but it's not true. This is a very effective way to stop this challenge and it does not cause a horse to become head-shy.) If you're not quick enough to bop him in the mouth, give him a hard smack on his neck.

- **Challenge: Biting.** Correction: This is the time to get incredibly mean and scary. Give your horse the impression you're going to kill him. Smack his neck three or four times as hard as you can, hard enough to hurt your own hand. If he bites you a second time, you weren't mean and scary enough the first time!

- **Challenge: Pushing you around with his head.** Correction: OK, sometimes this is really cute, but still... he can only push you if he's in your space, right? Make him step back.

- **Challenge: Your horse is herd-bound, which means he whinnies for other horses while he is with you.** Correction: Herd-bound horses are worried about their safety when they are away from other horses. As you develop your leadership skills, your horse will come to feel safe in your presence and the whinnying will eventually stop. Meanwhile, don't get distracted by it. Work harder to keep your horse's attention by focusing on getting him to do what you want him to do. Whatever you're asking your horse to do when he whinnies, challenge him to do it better. Or ask him to do something completely different, then something else besides that. Keep him too busy to worry about anything. Build a trusting, interesting relationship with your horse and the day will come when he will prefer to spend more time with you than with other horses.

Chapter Eight

A LEADER PREPARES her HERD in ADVANCE

The kindest thing you can do for your horse is to allow him the opportunity to calmly submit to your leadership before you hop on to ride. If he knows you're the leader beforehand, he can relax and enjoy himself. He's happy to carry you around as long as you carry the responsibility of leadership. Groundwork is your opportunity to get your horse calm, attentive and cooperative before you climb in the saddle. Groundwork before riding gets your rides off to a safe start.

Since your goal is to get your horse calm, attentive and cooperative, be aware of his body language and actions during the exercises. If he is holding his head high, he's not very relaxed. If he's not looking at you or turning an ear toward you, he's not giving you his full attention. If he doesn't do what you ask, he's not giving you his full cooperation. Your horse will not just hand these things over to you; you have to work through the exercises to earn his attention and cooperation. As you do that, your horse will start to lower his head as he relaxes under your leadership.

Begin all of the groundwork exercises with your dressage whip in hand and the lead chain fastened over the nose band of your horse's halter. If an exercise is particularly difficult, keep an eye on your horse's mouth and work through the exercise until your horse starts licking and chewing. This is a sign that your horse is starting to submit to your leadership in that exercise.

Your body language tells your horse how you feel about being the leader, so it's important you use your body to convey your message. Even if you don't feel confident, try to look like you do. When you want your horse out of your space, stand upright and square shouldered to look as bold and intimidating as possible. When you want to invite your horse into your space, soften your posture by rounding your shoulders and tipping your head to the side. When you ask your horse to face you, maintain eye contact with him to encourage him to pay attention to you.

Rhythm is the Foundation of Calmness When you do your groundwork exercises, it is not enough just to ask your horse to walk or trot. Whatever the gait, it's important that you get him to move in a forward steady rhythm that is energetic but not rushed. Pay attention to how fast he's going and don't just accept what he gives you. If he moves too slowly, speed him up. If he moves too quickly, slow him down. Setting his rhythm is key to getting him to come into a state of calmness.

Giving the Aids When you want your horse to do something, you have to give him an aid (the correct signal) to do it. Aids have stages. Give an aid very gently at first. If your horse doesn't respond, apply the aid with more force or more drama. If your horse still doesn't respond, you have to come with as much force or drama as necessary to get your horse to respond. You have to be fair about giving aids, but you also have to prove to your horse that you are the leader. When it comes to giving aids, impress upon your horse that you're willing to ask him nicely, but you're not going to beg him to do something.

Reward Instantly As soon as your horse responds to an aid, you should reward him instantly. To do that, stop applying the aid the second you get the response you're looking for. It sounds really easy, but it takes a ton of awareness and practice to be able to do it. If you make it a habit to reward instantly, your horse will become very sensitive to your lightest aids. If you don't, your horse will get used to you applying aids over and over again and he will start to tune you out. He will become dull to your aids, so you will have to work harder and harder to get him to respond. That's no fun at all, so be aware of what you're doing and keep reminding yourself to reward instantly.

Exercise 1: Basic Leading

This exercise gets you thinking and acting like a leader by making your horse pay attention to you. If you get his full attention, he will move when you move, stop when you stop, and back when you back with no pressure on the lead rope. Begin this exercise with the whip in your left hand.

Start by leading your horse at a brisk pace to make sure he's keeping up with you. If he is lagging behind, stay back by his shoulder and reach your left hand back behind you to give him a little tap on his belly with the whip. He might shoot out in front of you the first couple of times you do this, but that's OK, just let him. He'll slow down after a couple of strides and you will need to tap him again. Just keep repeating until he understands that you want him to keep up with you.

Once you have your horse keeping up with you at a brisk pace, come to a quick stop. Your horse should halt at the exact same time you do. If he doesn't give a quick jerk and release on the lead. Try again, and if he shoots out in front of you a second time, increase your aid by giving a much sharper jerk and release on the lead. Repeat until he pays attention and stops right when you stop. Once he gets the idea, only give a correction if he puts pressure on the lead. Once you've achieved perfection at the walk, ask your horse to trot with you by gradually quickening your pace. Practice until your horse halts with you at both the walk and trot. Then, switch sides and practice this same exercise with your horse on your left.

For safe leading, double up the excess lead rope and drape it across the palm of your hand, as illustrated. Never allow the lead rope to loop around your hand.

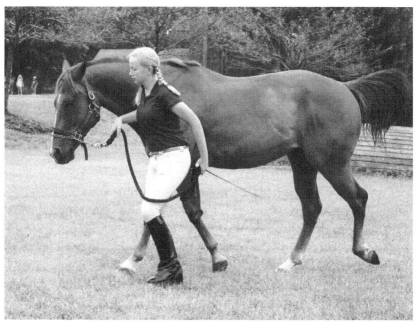

Claire gives Charlie a tap with the whip to cue him to trot. When she gets what she wants, she is careful to stop giving the aid and keeps the whip in a non-threatening position by her side. She will only raise it if he starts to lag behind. Notice she is not pulling on the lead but allowing it to hang gently.

Advance your skill by adding backing to the process. From the halt, stay facing forward, apply pressure on the lead and draw it to the center of your horse's chest as you begin to move backward. If he doesn't move with you, give little taps on his chest with the whip. Tap harder and harder until he starts to back, and then quit tapping all together.

It takes a few tries to get a horse to back straight up rather than veering off to the right. If your horse veers to the right, reach around his chest and press the whip to his right shoulder.

Once your horse is backing with you, start decreasing your aid. See if he will back with just a light tap, then just the indication that you are about to tap, then just the indication that you are about to back up. Practice until your horse backs with you with no pressure on the lead.

Left: When Charlie moves off to the right rather than straight back, Claire holds her ground and corrects him by pressing the whip to his right shoulder. Right: After a few attempts, Claire and Charlie back up together in a nice straight line.

Exercise 2: Making your Horse Stay Put

This exercise teaches you to define your space. With your horse on the lead line at a halt, stand in front of him facing him, tell him whoa, and then start moving backward. He will try to move with you, so jiggle the lead line and say "whoa" to signal him that you want him to stay put.

The further you move away from him, the more likely he is to move toward you; so be ready to jiggle the lead rope harder if you must. If he keeps advancing, lunge toward him as you jiggle the lead. Lunging toward him is using your body language to tell him to back off. Practice until you can get to the very end of the lead rope keeping your horse at a halt by barely jiggling the lead.

Now, invite your horse into your space by softening your posture and applying light steady pressure to the lead rope. Increase the amount of steady pressure as needed until he moves forward. If necessary, lean your full body weight against it. His forward motion will relieve the pressure on the lead, so the second he moves forward he's rewarded instantly. Practice until you can get your horse to come toward you with barely any pressure on the lead.

Advance your skill by asking your horse to take just one or two steps toward you, then make him halt by jiggling the lead rope. Practice until you can get your horse to halt just by lifting your hand as if you were going to jiggle the lead.

Set yourself up for success. When you're trying to get your horse to pay attention to you, make sure *you* maintain eye contact with your horse.

When Charlie attempts to move into Claire's space, she jiggles the lead line and moves toward him to get him to back up and stay put.

47

Since jiggling the lead line and waving her arms yielded no results, Maggie lunges toward Cooper to get him to back up. Be fair and gentle when giving an aid, but come with more force or drama when needed.

Exercise 3:
Making your Horse Back out of your Space

This exercise helps you further define your space. Stand out in front of your horse facing him. Start jiggling the lead rope, and keep jiggling it progressively harder and harder. As soon as your horse gives you any indication that he is about to move backward, immediately stop jiggling the lead to let him know that's exactly what you want him to do.

If you are jiggling the lead rope with all your might and your horse is giving you no indication that he's about to budge, you have to do whatever it takes to make him budge. Lunge at him, throw your arms up, make him move.

Once you get your horse thinking backward, wait a couple of seconds and then start the exercise again. Start out softly and increase the jiggling as needed, but this time stop the jiggling when he takes a full step backward. Again, wait a few seconds to allow him to let this sink in, then start the exercise again. When your horse takes a full step back, continue jiggling the lead softly till you get a second step. Then a third step, and so on. Always make sure you give your horse enough lead to allow him to back up. Practice this exercise until you can make your horse back out of your space by jiggling the lead as softly as possible.

Combine this with the previous exercise and practice until you get really good moving your horse into and out your space, and getting him to halt and stay put.

> If you have to use a lot of drama to back a horse out of your space, he might be a little hesitant the first time you invite him back into your space. Don't worry, he'll come. He just needs a second to process his newfound respect for you.

Exercise 4:
Getting your Horse Sensitive to a Light Touch

This exercise teaches you that you should not have to shove your full body weight into a horse to get him to move his various body parts. He should move when you ask him politely.

Stand by your horse and lightly touch his hip with your finger tips to ask him to move his butt away from you. If he doesn't budge, steadily apply more pressure, digging in with your thumb if necessary. The second he moves, reward instantly by removing the pressure. Now repeat the exercise, again starting with very light pressure and applying more only if needed. Practice until your horse steps away from your very light touch. Move to the other side of your horse's body and repeat the process.

To get him to move his shoulders, start with your fingertips on his shoulder. To get him to move both his front and back end at the same time, start with your finger tips on his ribs in the center of his body. To get him to move backward, start with your fingertips on his chest. Practice until your horse steps away from your lightest possible touch.

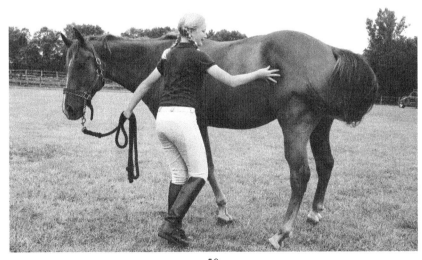

Exercise 5:
Making your Horse Move Out and Around you, Halt, and Change Directions

This exercise allows you to establish a lot of control of your horse on the ground, before you have to establish control of him in the saddle. Start this exercise on the left side of your horse, with the lead in your left hand and the whip in your right hand. Facing the center of your horse's body, put yourself in position so that your horse's head, his hind end, and you form a triangle. To signal him to move, point him off to the left as you raise the whip toward his hind end. If he doesn't move, give a little tap with the whip, increasing the force of the aid until he moves. As soon as he moves, lower the whip and allow him to travel in a circle around you.

In this exercise, he will probably challenge you first by coming right at you with his shoulder to see if he can move you out of your space, so plant your feet in one spot and hold your ground. Push him away by waiving your lead rope hand up toward his face, or by giving him a hard tap on his shoulder with the whip. The whole point is he has to move out around you, not the other way around.

The second challenge he might present is that he will decide to change directions all on his own. Don't let him. Keep him moving to the left and if you sense he's about to stop, raise the whip toward his hind end. If you're not quick enough, he will stop, but to change directions he will have to turn to face you so stop him right there. Point off to the left again, and give him a tap on his shoulder with the whip. Practice until you can keep him moving consistently in this one direction.

The third challenge he might present is that he will decide to trot rather than walk. Pull him into a tighter circle to make it uncomfortable for him to trot. The fourth challenge is that he will try to walk very, very slowly. Give him a little tap with the

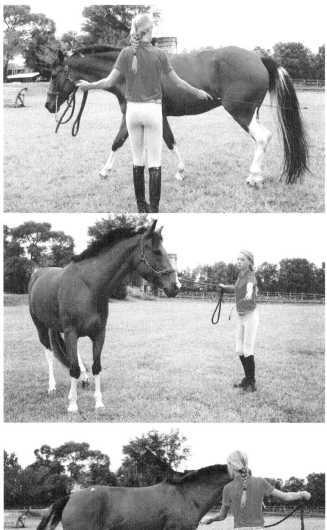

Top: Riley raises the whip to ask Prince to walk. Center: Riley asks for a change of direction by switching the whip and lead to opposite hands, and then raising the whip as she pulls Prince's head toward her. Bottom: She reminds Prince to stay out of her space by pointing the whip toward his shoulder.

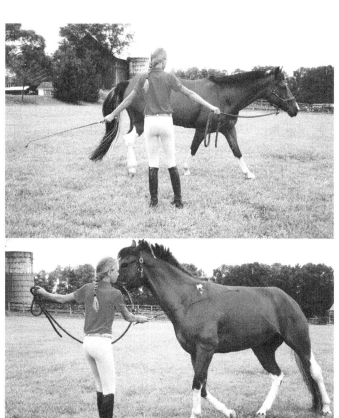

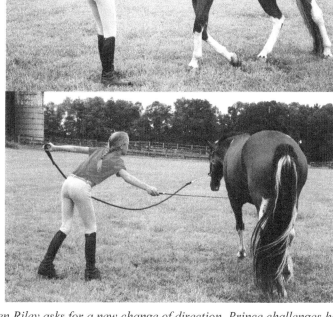

When Riley asks for a new change of direction, Prince challenges her by speeding up and attempting to charge into her space. She protects herself by popping his shoulder solidly with the whip. She then claims her space more assertively by lunging toward Prince.

53

whip to speed him up. If he trots, slow him down and then re-peat the process. Make him walk, but just a little faster than he wants to. Before making him halt, switch hands with your lead rope and whip. To get the halt, pull on the lead rope to make him turn his face toward you as you say "whoa." If he keeps walking, pull him closer to you and reach the whip right out in front of his face to stop his forward motion. If he acts like he doesn't see the whip, swish it back and forth to make a wall in front of his face.

Now make him move off to the right. Since he's already facing you, point him off to the right as you raise the whip toward his shoulder. If he doesn't move, tap his shoulder with the whip. As he moves off in the new direction remain aware for any challenges he may present. Again, before making him halt, switch hands with your lead rope and whip.

As you get your horse moving out and around you, be aware of what your feet are doing. They shouldn't be walking all around, but rather just pivoting in one spot. The point of this exercise is for you to stay put while your horse moves out and around you. Practice until you can make your horse move around you with ease. Once you get use to this exercise, start decreasing your aids. Try not raising the whip so high and work toward not having to raise it at all. See if you can get him moving simply by pointing left or right. For the halt, use the whip as an aid only if needed. The first time you get a really decent halt (prompt and with almost no pressure on the lead rope) take a moment to reward your horse with a nice rub on his neck. Then continue on to see if you can get him to halt from your voice alone.

Advance your skill by making your horse go over obstacles – trot poles, cavaletti, etc. When you are comfortable with this exercise at the walk and trot, grab a lunge line and lunge whip and advance to canter. As your skills improve, try mixing up the transitions. Instead of just halt to walk to trot to canter, try halt to trot, canter to halt, walk to canter, and so forth.

Exercise 6:
Circling your Horse to Make Sure you
Have his Attention

This exercise proves how well you're doing as the leader. As the follower, your horse should pay attention to you and only you. So, when you put him in one spot and make a wide circle around him, he should pivot to maintain eye contact with you. Try this exercise at the end of your groundwork.

From the halt, make your horse stay put as you move away from him. Maintain eye contact and start walking in a wide circle around him. If he tries to advance toward you, jiggle the lead rope to let him know you want him to stay put and just pivot. If he does not attempt to pivot, pull his head around to let him know that's what you want him to do. This might coax him to advance toward you, but just jiggle the lead rope to tell him to stay back. Once your horse starts pivoting, try moving faster. If you have your horse's attention, he will pivot as quickly as necessary to maintain the eye contact with you.

As your leadership skills improve, your horse will start paying more attention to you. His ear will turn toward you and stay turned toward you for longer periods of time; and he will start maintaining eye contact - first with just one eye, then both. These are signs that you are on the right track.

Many people think horses are happy when their ears are pointed forward, but really horses point their ears toward whatever has their interest. To get your horse's 'happy ears' on you, make yourself more interesting than anything or anyone else around.

Prince pivots to maintain eye contact with Riley as she runs in a large circle around him. She definitely has his attention.

Exercise 7:
Getting your Horse to Stand Still for Mounting

If your horse has a habit of moving when you mount, do groundwork with him to make sure he is calm and relaxed under your leadership before you attempt to mount. When you go to mount, help your horse keep his balance my making certain he is standing squarely underneath himself. If not, you can reach up on the saddle and rock his body from side to side to encourage him to adjust his weight evenly, or you can make him back up and move forward until he stands square. Now, say "whoa" firmly and then step your foot into the stirrup and swing your weight up to the center of the saddle as if you're going to mount, but don't put your leg over unless he stands

still. Just balance there for a moment. If your horse moves the slightest bit, hop off and make him back up until he tries to avoid going backward by moving forward or sideways. Pretend to mount again, and if he moves, repeat the backing. It won't take him long to figure out you want him to stand perfectly still while you mount.

When you mount, always make sure to position yourself over the center of the saddle, as Delaney illustrates, to help your horse keep his balance.

Chapter Nine

A LEADER PREVENTS HERD ANXIETY

Spooking causes more fear in riders and more injury to riders than just about anything else. Lead horses are responsible for all of the decisions about safety, which means lead horses must be on the lookout for danger. So much spooking takes place because riders do not take the lead position, thereby forcing their horses to look around for danger. If a horse spooks a lot, he apparently finds a lot of things dangerous.

Dealing effectively with your horse's common challenges will help stop much of the spooking because it helps prove to him that you are the leader. When your horse is no longer the leader, he becomes the follower. The follower's job is to pay attention to the leader. If your horse is paying attention to you, he won't have much time to look around for danger, will he?

When your horse gets scared, your initial response should always be to divert his attention back to you. Most riders wait until their horse is in a full blown panic to practice this, only to find out that it's almost impossible to get a panicked horse's attention. However, if you practice now with bomb-proofing exercises, you and your horse won't ever have to reach the panic stage.

The following chapter is an introduction to bomb-proofing. Bomb-proofing exercises are designed to build trusting relationships between horse and rider. The rider learns to focus and stay calm in order to gain their frightened horse's attention; and the horse learns that he can trust his rider to lead him safely through scary situations. If you do enough bomb-proofing, in even the scariest of situations, your horse will turn his attention to you and allow you to guide him rather than bolt. It's not called bomb-proofing for nothing.

Meanwhile, there are many other things you should do to prevent your horse from becoming a spooky horse. First and foremost, understand that it is your job to be aware of any danger that could harm you and your horse, and it is your horse's job to pay attention to you. As the leader, you must act as the stabilizing force when your horse gets scared. Your initial response always should be to act quickly to divert his attention back to you.

Horses present a lot of drama when they get frightened. Don't get sucked into the drama because it will destroy your horse's trust in your leadership. That means don't coddle your horse when he acts nervous and don't turn your attention to whatever scares him.

- Coddling (patting and talking to the horse in a soothing voice) is a reward in and of itself because it feels good. If you coddle your horse when he spooks, you are actually rewarding him for spooking. Horses tend to repeat the behaviors they get rewarded for. Don't get sucked into the drama and coddle your horse when he spooks. Rather, your response should be some type of reprimand, something that says, "Knock it off, you're just fine."

- If you turn your attention toward something that scared your horse, you are no longer in the lead – your horse is because you are allowing yourself to get distracted by his drama. Remember, it's the leader's job to be aware of any threats. What threats are in your area? Don't get sucked into the drama and start looking around to see what scared him – unless, of course, a mountain lion or bear is your immediate vicinity.

- The worst thing you can do is stop what you are doing to make your horse look at the scary thing. You may think you're taking charge, but in actuality you give up leading the moment you stop what you are doing to have your horse look at something you already know isn't going to hurt him. That's getting sucked into the drama waist deep. Plus, you'll be approving your horse's decision to look around for scary stuff rather than paying attention to you. It's your job to be aware of threats, not his.

Riders who get sucked into the drama create spooky horses. Whether you are on the ground or in the saddle, if your horse spooks, act quickly to divert his attention back to you.

WHEN LEADING

1. Think positively. Thoughts create energy and your horse feels your energy. If you think your horse ought to be afraid of something, you will cause him to be afraid of it. You have to be cool with everything if you want your horse to be cool with everything. Even if he's initially afraid of something, you can get him to be cool with it but the transformation starts in *your* head.

2. Get in the habit of keeping a chain over your horse's nose until the time comes when you are positive you can lead him past something scary without getting trampled and without losing control of him.

3. Horses have a tendency to get spooked by anything out of the norm, so be aware of your surroundings. Always try your best to keep yourself between your horse and an object that may startle him. That way, if he shies away from it, he won't be crowding *into* your space but rather *away* from your space.

4. Understand that your horse is big and it takes very little effort for him to barrel his weight right through you. He won't mean to, but your horse will run you over to get away from something that scares him - unless he's more afraid of you. Be vigilant about making your horse respect your space, *especially* when he's frightened.

61

Top: If Rachel had been at Oliver's shoulder, she could easily have gotten crushed when he spooked. Be aware of your surroundings. Bottom: If you think something up ahead might spook your horse, keep yourself safely between your horse and that object, noise or commotion.

If he crowds your space when he is scared, get seriously mean and scary and don't think twice about it. Do whatever it takes to convince your horse that *you*, when in danger of getting crushed, are the scariest thing he will ever encounter. Jerk the chain hard three or four times, with all your might if you have to, to get him out of your space. And then don't back off, which means don't let him creep back into your space after your initial reprimand. Put yourself between the horse and the object and force him to follow obediently behind you until he walks calmly.

WHEN RIDING

1. Understand that when you are riding your horse is not supposed to be looking all around. He is supposed to be paying attention to you. Make sure you're both on the same page about this by doing groundwork with him prior to mounting.

2. Be proactive by being aware of your surroundings. If you think something up ahead might spook your horse, don't avoid it but rather keep his attention focused on you and don't let him look at it as you draw near. You have his attention if at least one of his ears is turned toward you.

    a. If you do not have his attention, do not make a bee line for the scary thing. Start riding in circles keeping all your attention focused on riding the most perfect circles ever, which means using a stronger inside leg. This will cause you to focus on what you're doing, which is the only way you will be able to get your horse focused on you and away from the scary object.

    b. When you are confident you have your horse's attention, keep riding your perfect circles as you spiral your way toward the item. Be aware of your horse's body language because he'll let you know if he is still concerned about the item. The first sign will be both of his ears pointing toward it. The second sign is that he will try to turn his head to look at it while leaning his shoulder away from it. When he presents these signs, don't move any closer. Just keep him circling right there for a minute or two, ride harder and keep his head turned away from the item. To lean his shoulder away from the item, he must lean it onto your leg. Your leg is your space, so use your whip or crop to tap his shoulder out of your space. Work to get his full attention on you.

c. When you get your horse calm and attentive in that spot, ride off in the opposite direction for a minute or two. The 'riding away' part is crucial because it builds your horse's trust in your leadership. You have to ride away to give him time to process the fact that getting close to the scary thing didn't kill him. The 'riding away' is what allows you to move your horse closer to the item on the next approach. Take your time and pass by the item only when you are confident you can keep your horse calm and attentive as you ride by. If you aren't confident you can do that, wait until the day you are. Good leadership is always self-preservation at its best!

d. After riding safely past the item in one direction, don't take it for granted that your horse won't freak out at it when you change directions. Horse's eyes are very far apart. Even though he's seen the item with one eye, it will be a whole new experience for him when he sees it with his other eye. School him the exact same way in both directions.

3. If something takes you and your horse by surprise and he bolts away, you have not done your bomb-proofing. Like I said, it's not called bomb-proofing for nothing. Prevent bolting by bomb-proofing!

Top: Apache tells Madison he is concerned about the tarp through his body language—his ears point toward it and his shoulder moves away from it. Center: Madison keeps his head turned away from the tarp as she moves him closer to it. Bottom: She rewards Apache with a pat as they ride past the tarp without incident.

Top and center: As Madison schools past the tarp at a trot, her job is to maintain focus while Rachel gets progressively more distracting with the tarp. Bottom: Madison gives Apace plenty of rein when she feels confident he will trot past the tarp calmly. She knows she still has his attention because his ear is turned toward her.

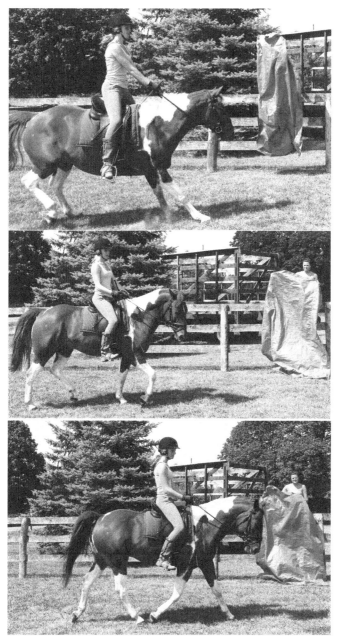

Top: When Madison changes directions Apache acts like he's never seen the tarp before. Center: On her second approach, Madison keeps Apache's head turned well away from the tarp. Meanwhile, Rachel has stopped waving the tarp to allow Madison time to establish control of her horse. Bottom: Madison gives more rein as Apache starts to relax.

67

Chapter Ten

A LEADER PRIMES her HERD for ACTION

Taking your horse through frequent bomb-proofing exercises is the quickest way to develop your leadership skills and build a more trusting partnership between you and your horse. I often hear people say that their horses spook and bolt 'right out of the blue for no reason what-so-ever.' Horses don't bolt for no reason. They bolt because they are put in the lead position and given no other option.

If something takes your horse by surprise, he might flinch or jump, but he is only going to bolt if he thinks his safety is in jeopardy. As the leader, you are responsible for the safety of you and your horse. Bomb-proofing allows you an opportunity to prove to him that you take this responsibility seriously. Take time to build a trusting relationship and, when frightened, your horse will allow you to protect him rather than bolt away to protect himself.

Frightened horses present all kinds of drama. To lead your horse safely through this world, you must learn to calmly and confidently deal with his drama so neither of you get hurt. Bomb-proofing teaches you to recognize your horse's fear while it is in its earliest stages – when he presents some drama but not enough to put the two of you in danger. It's during these moments that you can get your horse to pay attention to you so you can prove to him that his safety is not in jeopardy. Once he realizes that, he will calm down.

When you get the desired calmness, you must take your horse away from the scary situation for a few minutes to let him process the fact that the experience was a little scary but it didn't hurt him. This retreat is so important because it gives your horse time to build the self-confidence he needs to approach the situation again. Building your horse's self-confidence builds his trust in you. Building trust is crucial to you actually *becoming* your horse's leader. Building a trusting relationship with your horse is what lets you safely *stretch* your horse's comfort zone as far as you like, so the amount of fun the two of you can have together will be limited only by your imagination.

Bomb-proofing is about building your confidence in dealing with your horse's fear so that you can help him build confidence. Bomb-proofing is such a win/win situation for both horse and rider it's crazy not to do it.

Important Tips for Bomb-Proofing Exercises

- Always practice in an enclosed area so your horse can't go very far if he pulls the lead out of your hand. If this happens, don't get sucked into his drama. Stop what you are doing long enough to get control of your horse, and then continue doing exactly what you were doing before he got away from you.

- Strive to create only as much excitement as you can safely handle. Only you know your comfort level, so start with baby steps. As you proceed, your confidence will grow and you will be able to challenge both yourself and your horse more.

- Be direct and rhythmic in your mannerisms when introducing new items to your horse. You're trying to convince him he doesn't need to be afraid of stuff, so don't handle the items tentatively as if he *should* be afraid of them.

- When you rub your horse with an item, use the same type of comfortable pressure you use when brushing him. A nice firm rub feels good to just about any horse, while a tickly hesitant rub just feels creepy.

- Since we are used to leading horses on our right, it's easier to start the bomb-proofing exercises with your horse on your right. When you get more comfortable with the whole process, try starting new exercises with your horse on your left.

- Train both sides of your horse. Anything you do on the left side of his body you must duplicate on the right side of his body.

- Horses shy *away* from scary items. Until you're confident you can keep your horse out of your space, keep yourself between the horse and the item.

- At some point in your riding adventures, something will probably startle your horse while you're on his back. When that happens, the best possible thing he could do is flinch or freeze (spook in place) and then wait for you to tell him what to do next. During bomb-proofing, once your horse gains some trust in your leadership, he will start to spook in place. The first few times he does it, stop what you're doing for a few seconds and reward him with a nice rub to let him know that's exactly what you want him to do anytime he gets startled. The more trusting he becomes of your leadership, the less spooking he will do in general.

To begin the bomb-proofing exercises, you will need your longer halter training whip with the plastic flag taped to the end and your tarp. Be sure to fasten the lead chain over the nose band of your horse's halter to help you maintain control of your horse.

Detail of flagged whip.

Exercise 1: Introducing the Flagged Whip

Purpose: Since you will be putting your horse in frightening situations during bomb-proofing, it is very important that you protect your space so you don't get hurt. Taping a plastic flag to the end of your whip will allow you to guard your space more effectively because it makes the whip scarier to your horse. Therefore, introducing the flagged whip to your horse is a bomb-proofing exercise in and of itself and it teaches you how to introduce your horse to any item that frightens him.

To introduce your horse to the flagged whip, pick it up holding the flag end of it in your hand. Position yourself in front of your horse's shoulder so he can't see the flag and begin to rub his shoulder with it. He will probably present some drama and move around to try to get away from it. Your job is to stay cool and calm despite the drama. Move with him, ignore the drama and do your best to keep the flag pressed to his shoulder. When he comes to a halt, rub his shoulder with it until he is completely calm, and then drop the whip and walk away for a minute to reward him for calming down.

Come back to the whip and repeat the process until he presents no drama when you pick up the whip and rub the flag on his shoulder. Once he is completely calm about that, start working your way backward to rub the flag on his belly and haunches. At this point, you can allow him to see what you're doing and allow him to sniff the flag if he wants to. If he presents any drama, keep doing what you're doing until he calms down. Then stop what you're doing, drop the whip and walk away to reward him for calming down. Repeat the process on the opposite side of his body.

When he is calm about all that, start picking up the whip by the handle. Stand close to him as you begin rubbing him with the flag, and then start moving out away from him as you continue the rubbing. Again, make sure you do this on both sides of his body. Your goal is to be able to walk over to the whip, pick it

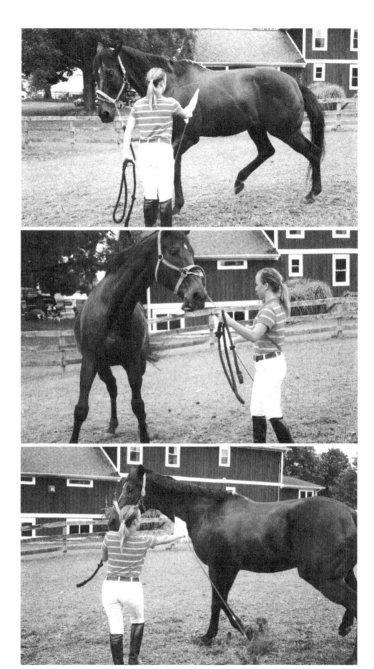

Top and center: Cooper is nervous about the flag, so when he steps away and catches sight of it his fear escalates. Bottom: Despite the drama, Maggie puts the flag right back on his shoulder and holds it there until he calms down.

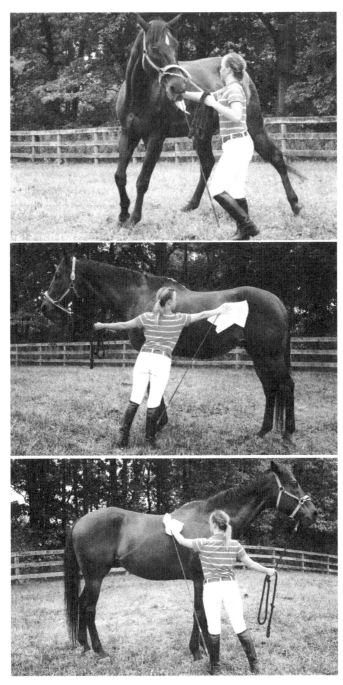

Since Maggie proved the flag wouldn't hurt him, Cooper now trusts her enough to let her rub it over both sides of his body.

74

up, and reach right out and rub him all over with the flag while he remains perfectly calm. Once you reach that point, have him circle out around you changing directions several times to get him used to doing groundwork with the flagged whip. If he presents any drama, it's important for you to stay focused and keep asking him to do what you want. By staying focused, you will be able to work him through his drama to calmness.

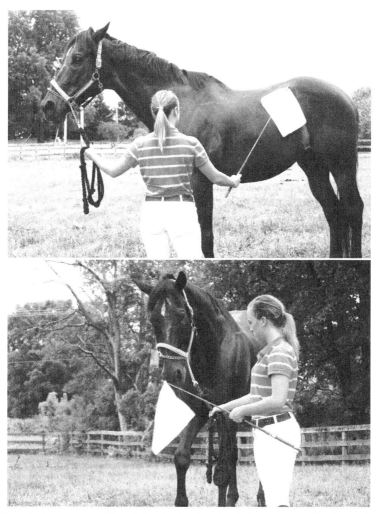

Maggie does an excellent job of using her body language to display calm, confident leadership with Cooper, who now seems to be more curious about the flag than afraid of it.

Top: When Maggie starts groundwork, Cooper gets nervous about the flag all over again, which is perfectly normal. To a horse, being introduced to the flagged whip and being asked to do groundwork with it are two completely different experiences. Bottom: As Maggie holds onto Cooper, she lowers the whip and carries it in a non-threatening position. Had she kept it raised, Cooper may have completely freaked out and gotten away from her. Be smart about creating only as much excitement as you can handle!

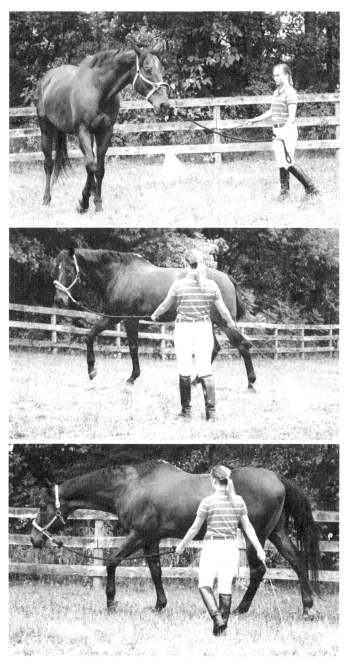

By maintaining her focus and not getting sucked into the drama, Maggie brings Cooper into a state of calmness, as evidenced by his head dropping lower and lower during the groundwork session.

Exercise 2: Introducing the Tarp

Purpose: This exercise exposes your horse to noise and commotion to teach you that you don't have to be quiet or tip-toe around him. ***Goal:*** To make as much noise and commotion as possible with the tarp while your horse stands perfectly calm.

To begin the exercise, the tarp should be folded up small to be as non-threatening as possible. Calmly lead your horse to the tarp, pick it up, and introduce it to him the same way you introduced the flagged whip, starting at his shoulder and working your way over the rest of his body. If he presents any drama, keep rubbing him in that spot until he calms down, and then drop the tarp and walk away.

When your horse is calm about that, start making the exercise more challenging for both of you. Each time you come back to the tarp, unfold it a little bit so it gets bigger each time you pick it up, and start shaking it out before you start rubbing him with it. Start making more noise with it when you rub it around on his body. Start draping it across his neck and back.

Work toward your horse remaining calm while you shake out the tarp really hard and toss it right up over his neck and back like a cooler. Prepare to pull the tarp off over his head by first pulling it back and forth over his ears a few times. When he is calm about that, pull it off over his head in a quick smooth motion. (Making your horse back up during this process helps prevent too much drama.) Practice until your horse remains calm about it. To increase the challenge, practice pulling it over his head more and more slowly.

> When introducing a new item to your horse, it's very important you handle the item matter-of-factly. If you handle it hesitantly as if your horse *should* be afraid of it, he *will* be afraid of it.

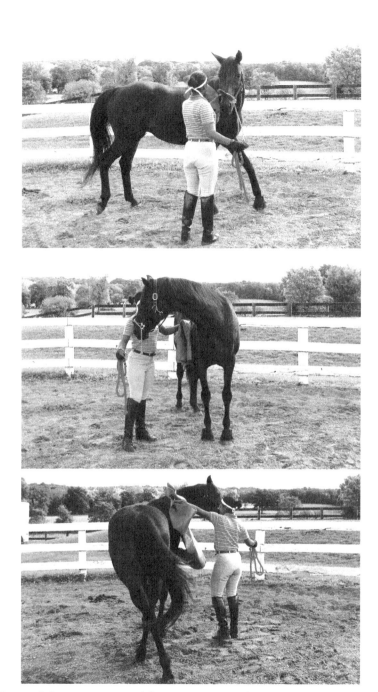

Top and Center: Unsure of the tarp, Koga circles around to avoid it. Remaining calm, Stormy holds the tarp in place until he comes to a halt. Bottom: The circling begins again as Stormy allows the tarp to expand.

Top photo: Kyliegh allows Ice Baby to watch her drape the tarp over his back. It's fine to allow your horse to satisfy his curiosity about objects when he isn't presenting any drama about them. Bottom photo: Ice Baby is only slightly concerned when Kyleigh shakes out the tarp in front of him.

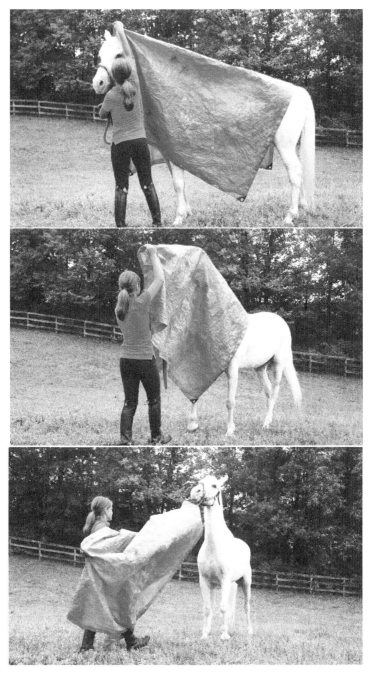

Kyleigh gets Ice Baby used to the feeling of the tarp around his ears before she pulls it off over his head.

81

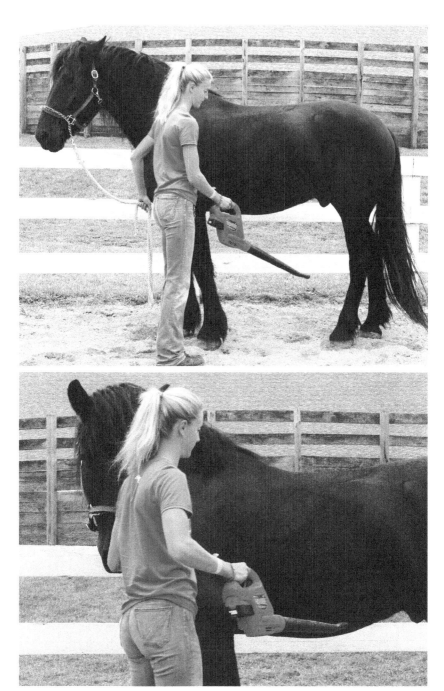

Use your imagination and introduce your horse to all kinds of stuff. Here, Tina helps Cinder make friends with the leaf blower.

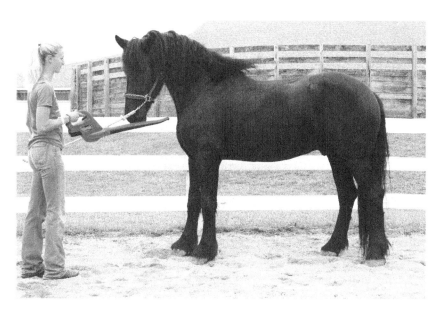

To introduce your horse to items that blow or spray, allow your horse to get used to the sensation a tiny bit at a time. Start at the back toward his hind feet and work your way forward and up.

By rewarding with treats, Tina makes this an extra positive experience for Cinder—one he clearly seems to be enjoying!

Exercise 3: Walking with the Tarp

Purpose: This exercise teaches you to make your horse move calmly under your leadership despite noise and commotion. *Goal:* For your horse to remain calm while carrying the tarp, and while it slips off his back.

With the tarp unfolded the entire way, drape it over your horse like a blanket. Start walking while keeping your horse by your side. If he tries to shoot out in front of you, correct him with the lead chain. As you are walking around, reach back and pull the tarp off of him. Let it drop to the ground and continue walking. When he is calm about that process, drape the tarp over him allowing half of it to hang over his hind end so it will eventually fall off on its own as you walk around. Take off walking again, and as soon as the tarp slips off, come to a halt. If your horse presents drama or tries to step away from the tarp, correct him with the lead chain. Make him stand calm for a few seconds, and then reward him by walking away. Repeat the process until he is no longer nervous about carrying the tarp or the tarp falling off his back, and he comes to halt calmly and promptly when directed.

To increase the challenge, practice this exercise using other items; anything that's flat enough to stay on your horse's rear end for at least a few steps—dressage cones, buckets, cardboard boxes, etc.

> Calm horses don't just happen. They are created when riders take the time to build trusting relationships with their horses. Bomb-proofing is a surprisingly simple yet amazingly effective way to build a trusting relationship with your horse.

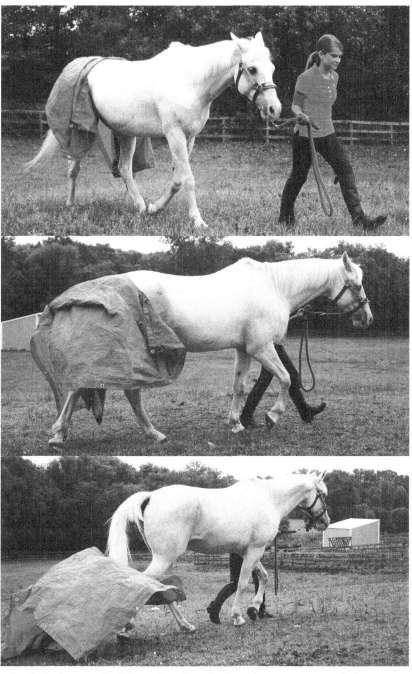

Ice Baby has reached the point where he is no longer concerned about carrying the tarp and presents no drama when it slips to the ground.

Stormy gets Koga used to carrying the tarp overhead. Use your imagination to build your horse's trust.

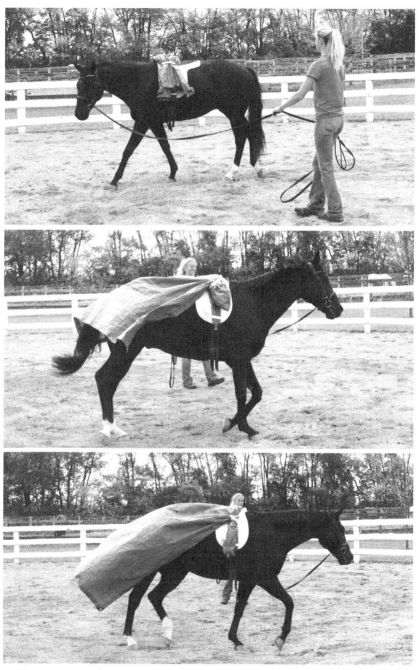

Using a circingle, Tina gets creative with the tarp letting out the length in small increments until Beau is caped like a superhero. Taking it step by step, you can get your horse used to anything.

Exercise 4: Crossing Over the Tarp

Purpose: This exercise teaches you to use the approach and retreat method to get your horse to walk over something scary. *Goal:* To get your horse to calmly walk across the tarp.

Be certain you're able to make your horse come toward you and back up before starting this exercise. (Groundwork Exercise 3.) Some horses are inclined to jump forward to get off the tarp which puts the handler in danger of getting run over. Making your horse back up allows you to control his forward motion and forces him to pay more attention to you than the tarp. Keep your flagged whip in hand to enforce the backing if needed. During this exercise, take your time and achieve complete calmness before proceeding to the next step.

Lead your horse to the tarp, shake it out really hard, and spread it flat on the ground. (Note: if there is a breeze, weight the corners of the tarp to prevent it from blowing around.) Step onto the tarp and walk all around on it to let your horse see it isn't dangerous, and then walk away. Lead your horse back toward the tarp. When you reach the point where he is hesitant to go any further, go out in front of him, stand on the tarp and ask him to take one more step toward you. As soon as he takes the one step forward, immediately back him up and walk away as a reward.

If your horse tries to back up instead of stepping forward, you will have a hard time stopping him because of his strength. In order to make it clear to him that he is not allowed to back without your permission, move toward him while he is backing and give a couple of hard jerks on the lead chain. If that isn't enough, increase the reprimand by tapping him on his chest with the whip, and then make him back up a few more steps than he originally wanted to. The point is to get your horse thinking less about the tarp and more about doing what you ask.

Once you have your horse stepping forward when you ask him

to, keep leading him to the tarp until he is close enough to sniff it. Allow him to sniff around for a few seconds, and then back him up and walk away. On your next approach, in order for him to take a step closer to you, he will have to step onto the tarp. As soon as he steps one hoof onto the tarp, back him off and walk away. Approach again, and this time ask him to step both front hooves onto the tarp, and then back him off and walk away. Then three hooves, then four, backing him up and walking away in between.

Once he is calm putting all four hooves onto the tarp, ask him to take a couple of steps toward the center, then back him off the tarp and walk away. Then walk to the center, back off and walk away. Next, try to lead him across the tarp, but be ready to give a jerk on the lead if he tries to rush. Keep practicing until your horse is completely calm about following you across the tarp and standing in the center of it. While you practice, make sure to approach the tarp from different directions.

When you've gotten your horse used to calmly following you across the tarp, include the tarp in your groundwork exercises. Have him move out away from you and cross the tarp on his own from every direction. Work toward getting him to whoa in the center of the tarp. Set up a small jump at one end of the tarp and send him over it from both directions.

If you can't get your horse to cross the tarp the first time you try this exercise, don't lose patience, don't worry and don't give up. It takes time to develop a trusting relationship with your horse. As you work to improve your leadership skills in other areas, keep coming back to this exercise. It may take a couple of weeks to complete it. Just keep trying it *until* your horse follows you over the tarp.

Note: If your horse is hesitant about stepping into a horse trailer or a wash bay, use the method of having him step in one foot at a time to help him build confidence. Many horses move sideways to avoid going forward into a trailer. If your horse presents this challenge, use the whip to tap him back into position, and be sure to reprimand any unapproved backing.

When you are riding, use the approach and retreat method to build your horse's confidence and get him to cross bridges, streams, or anything else he might be hesitant to cross.

Opposite page: Anna leans her weight against the lead rope until Piper takes one step toward the tarp. Then Anna backs her away immediately to ensure Piper pays more attention to her than the tarp.

Above: By bringing Piper onto the tarp one hoof at a time, Anna gets Piper to walk over the tarp calmly.

Ice Baby is pretty concerned when Kyleigh picks up the tarp to drag it for the first time. By completely ignoring his drama, Kyleigh helps him calm down in just a few seconds.

Exercise 5: Dragging the Tarp

Purpose: This exercise teaches you to keep your horse following calmly despite noise and distraction coming from behind you. *Goal:* For your horse to remain calm as you drag the tarp behind him.

Before you begin this exercise, attach a string about 10 feet long to one corner of your tarp. Bailing twine is perfect for this. Lead your horse to the tarp; pick it up by the corner where the string is attached and allow it to drag along on the ground as you lead your horse around. He might try to dance away from you, so give jerks on the lead if he presents too much drama and just keep walking. As soon as he calms down, drop the tarp and walk away. Repeat the process until your horse is not displaying any nervous behavior at all while you drag the tarp around.

When you have reached that point, start letting out some of the string to allow the tarp to drag out further behind you. Work in increments allowing the tarp to drag further behind you each time until it eventually drags out behind your horse. Practice this exercise leading your horse from both sides of his body. To make sure he doesn't get tangled up with the tarp, when leading on his left, turn to the left; when leading on his right, turn to the right.

To increase the challenge, string twine through the eyelets of the tarp to make a sack and then toss in a variety of items that make different noises— a couple of empty buckets, a trash bag filled with empty soda cans, etc.

Back in the day, horses carried humans everywhere—including into battle where they were surrounded by gunfire and cannon shots. Carry that thought into your bomb-proofing sessions. Help your horse become your brave, loyal, bomb-proof partner.

93

Exercise 6: Moving your Horse Past the Tarp

Purpose: This exercise teaches you how to approach scary situations (objects, noises, etc.) with your horse and move him past them without bolting. You should use the same principal to move your horse past scary situations when riding.

You must drape your tarp over the fence for this exercise, so attempt it for the first time on a calm, non-windy day. To begin the exercise, stand well away from the tarp. Move your horse out and around you and have him change directions several times just to get him paying attention to you. Keep him paying attention to you as you start walking toward the tarp. As you advance, pay attention to your horse's body language because it will tell you when you are close enough to the tarp for your horse to be concerned about it. The first thing he will do is point his ears toward it, and if you get close enough he will lean his shoulder away from it.

As soon as his body language tells you he is concerned, stop advancing toward the tarp and work your horse in that spot until he focuses his attention back to you. To get him to forget about the tarp and pay attention to you, *you* **have to forget about the tarp** and make your horse pay attention to you. It's very important that you focus on making him do exactly what you want.

If he leans his shoulder toward you, point the whip toward it to remind him to stay out of your space. If needed, tap his shoulder with the whip. When he turns his ears toward the tarp, lift the whip or make him change directions to bring his focus back to you. Your goal is to get him to keep an ear on you as he passes by the tarp because this tells you that you have become more important to him than the tarp. When you get him to this point, bring him to a halt, give him a pat and walk away from the tarp.

Conduct your next approach in the same manner, but this time instead of walking away when you get his attention, take a couple of steps closer to the tarp. Get his full attention in that spot and then give him a retreat. Repeat the process, each time working your horse closer to the tarp. If he starts to rush, pull him toward you in a tight circle until he slows down, then send him back out again. Progress through this exercise in an approach and retreat manner until you can get your horse to calmly pass within inches of the tarp from both directions at both the walk and trot.

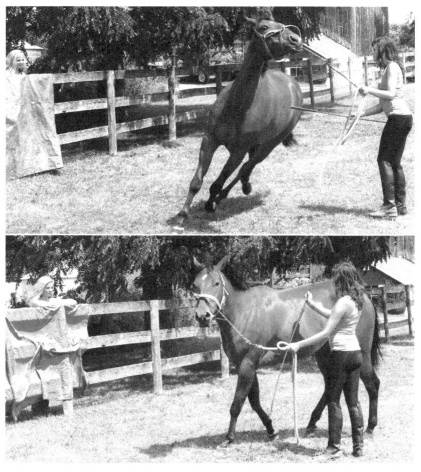

Top: To avoid the tarp, Oliver leans his shoulder toward Rachel and rushes past it. As Rachel works to slow him down, she protects her space by giving him a jab with the handle of the whip. Bottom: Once she's made her point, Rachel is now able to keep Oliver out of her space with gentle reminders.

To increase the challenge, attempt this exercise on a breezy day while the tarp blows about in the wind—just be sure to secure the tarp to the fence so it can't blow away.

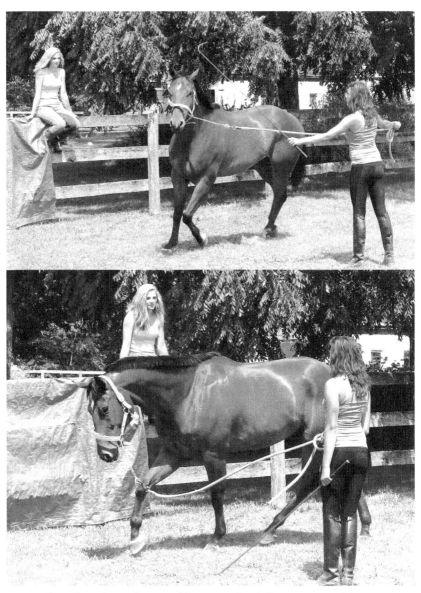

Top: By asking for a change of direction, Rachel encourages Oliver to pay attention to her—not the tarp. Bottom: Once very nervous about the tarp, Oliver now walks past it calmly, with head low and an ear toward Rachel.

Purpose: This exercise teaches you to stay calm and focused no matter what's going on. ***Goal:*** To keep your horse calm and attentive to you despite another person creating a distraction with the tarp. Enlist the help of your instructor or a fellow rider for this exercise.

To begin the exercise, your assistant should pick a spot to stand in that is well away from you and your horse and allow you to work your horse toward her. Starting out a little conservatively in the beginning, she should work toward creating as much distraction as possible by waving the tarp, shaking it out, swinging it around her head, etc.

Your job is to make your horse forget about the tarp and pay attention to you as you work him closer and closer to the distraction. Get him doing all of the groundwork exercises. Mix things up and keep him busy so he has to focus on you. The entire time, be aware of his body language so you can help him through any fear while it's in its earliest stage. Use the same approach and retreat method that you learned in the previous exercises to build his confidence. Once you get your horse fairly close to the distraction, test your leadership skills by seeing if you can get him to stand calmly facing away from it. Further test your skills by seeing if you can get him to calmly back up toward it.

To increase the challenge, have your assistant walk all around to create distraction in different areas and at intermittent times.

PRACTICE! Don't let a preventable accident come between you and your horse. Prepare your herd for anything through frequent bomb-proofing sessions.

Above: Anna develops her ability to focus while Stormy does her best to distract her and Piper with the tarp. Opposite Page: Katie hones her focusing skills with her sister Tina's help.

The "distractor's" job is start out conservatively and get progressively louder, crazier, and more obnoxious... so as to be as distracting as possible. (Tina liked the job so much she caused equipment failure!)

Lexie spends time getting Izzy comfortable with the tarp on his second day of bomb-proofing under saddle.

Bomb-Proofing Continued

Now that you have the tools and information you need to complete several bomb-proofing exercises, you are well on your
way to achieving a new level of trust with your horse. Remember to be patient and not rush through any exercises in this
book. Your horse will tell you when he is ready to move on, so
just keep listening to him.

Since you know how to introduce your horse to scary items,
don't let him go through life being afraid of things. Build his
confidence by introducing him to umbrellas, giant stuffed animals, plastic bags, beach balls, anything and everything. Be
creative.

Develop you ability to focus and keep your horse calm no matter what. Get together with other riders for bomb-proofing ses-

*Build your confidence on the ground before bomb-proofing in the saddle.
Above: Katie lets Miss Major (aka Chubby) check out the umbrella.*

*Lexie makes sure Izzy is cool with the bag of empty soda cans
before riding off with it.*

sions on a regular basis and take turns providing distractions for each other. Bring in different items to create the distractions. Remember to be creative. Horses that are exposed to lots of things find out that few pose any danger. Baby strollers, pool toys, floats, and giant pieces of cardboard are just a few things you can use. If you plan to do any showing with your horse, set up a tent as a distraction since tents are seen at many shows.

And don't forget about the noise. While many horses are "sight" spookers, many others are "sound" spookers. Make lots of noise during your bomb-proofing sessions using anything you can find to make noise with. There are even CD's made especially for bomb-proofing that have all kinds of different sounds such as jackhammers, marching bands, people scream-ing and running around on metal bleachers, lions roaring, and more. Develop your ability to keep your horse calm on the ground first, and then begin bomb-proofing in the saddle.

By building his confidence step by step, Lexie helps Izzy remain steady even when she shakes the bag of soda cans with all her might.

In your daily life with your horse, always be aware of his body language so you can recognize and deal with any fear in its earliest stage.

Treat every fearful situation like a trust-building, confidence-boosting, bomb-proofing exercise to keep both you and your horse out of harm's way. The more you do this, the more your horse will come to seek and trust your guidance during scary situations and you will be able to respond in a way that continues to build his confidence.

You are the leader; never forget to act like one.

Happy *safe* riding!

REMEMBER:

A leader always proves she is the herd alpha!

Lexie continues bomb-proofing with help from her brother.
Above: Izzy is obviously concerned when Corey rattles the bag of empty
soda cans, so Lexie quickly diverts his attention and rides right past. Facing
Page: Corey has the art of distraction down to a science, but Lexie is a fo-
cusing machine and Izzy trusts her to keep him safe.

Bomb-proofing teaches you to keep yourself calm so you can keep your
horse calm no matter what!

Acknowledgements

The people at Thomet Stables offered me an overwhelming amount of encouragement and support while writing this book. You're all amazing, and I am deeply grateful to each and every one of you.

Holly Thomet, I appreciate you devoting so much time and energy to helping me see this book through to completion. From taking photographs, to editing, to obsessing over the title with me... thank you.

Rena Hays, you were the most phenomenal assistant. Thank you so much for always knowing what's needed ahead of time. What would I (or my sweatshirt) do without you? Thanks too for not only taking photographs, but for agreeing to be in some as well.

Jane Wheeler, thank you for getting the ball rolling. (I wonder if there's a rock song in that conversation we had???) Thank you too for editing and for bringing your horsemanship knowledge to the process.

Riley Bieker, Madison Collier, Kristen Eccleton, Rena Hays, Katie Mast, Tina Mast, Kyleigh Perski, Anna Petertyl, Emily Thomet, Olivia Thomet, Claire Reeves, Delaney Smits, Maggie Walters, Stormy M. Walters, Rachel Windas, Corey Wobma and Lexie Wobma: thank you all for being such wonderful models and for being incredibly fun to work with.

Phillip Sterling, I am very grateful to you for volunteering your time and professional expertise for this book's final phase of editing.

Bonnie West, where do I even begin? For your faith and confidence in me, for your wisdom and sage advice, for bringing your bizarre sense of humor to every situation... for *everything...* thank you.

Ben Thomet, thank you for your support on this project, but most of all, thanks for building a great barn and letting me do my thing there for so many years.

Gerald Richardson, thank you for listening to me talk about horses endlessly and for making me laugh constantly. Love you, baby!

CPSIA information can be obtained at www.ICGtesting.com
Printed in the USA
LVOW02s0731230714

395620LV00010B/81/P

9 781478 724865